GASLIGHTING

Recognize Manipulative and how to avoid the Gaslight Effect.

Narcissistic Abuse Recovery, Aggressive Narcissist, Personality disorder, Codependency, Empath, Covert Emotional Manipulation.

Jack Mind

Table of Contents

Introduction 7

Chapter 1. Gaslighting 10

Chapter 2. Understanding the Ins and Outs of Gaslighting 17

Chapter 3. How to spot a gaslighter 32

Chapter 4. Cognitive Dissonance | How Manipulation Affects You 35

   Effects of Manipulation 41

Chapter 5. How Gaslighting Narcissists operate to make their Victim Think that they are Crazy 49

   What Is A Narcissist? 49

   Narcissism and Gaslighting 51

      The Art of Making Others Crazy 53

      Making People do What the Narcissist Wants 55

Chapter 6. The Effects of Gaslighting 59

   Recovering from Gaslighting 60

   Are You Being Gas lighted? 60

   Gaslighting tends to work in stages 63

Chapter 7. Signs you are Being Manipulated with Gaslighting 65

Chapter 8. Things Narcissists Say During Gaslighting. 74

   Stuff Your Gaslighting Abuser Says 74

Chapter 9. Empowering Ways to Disarm a Narcissist and Take Control 77

Techniques to handle narcissists 77

Get away 77

Avoid the inner circle 78

Avoid narcissistic injury 80

Avoid exposing them 81

Admire and listen to them 81

Don't reject them 82

Avoid showing weakness 83

Give them an "out" 84

Don't expect fairness 85

They want to look good 85

Understand their narcissistic supply 86

An audience 87

Status 87

Sex 88

Love 88

Avoid flooding them with supply 89

Chapter 10. Ways to Stop a Deceiver in Their Tracks 90

Putting an End to Gaslighting 90

Change Is Possible 93

Born of Vulnerability 94

When the Narcissist Finds True, Secure Love 96

Breaking the Cycle 96

The Narcissist to who wants to Change 97

The Trouble with Emotional Abuse 100

Unmasking Emotional Abuse 101

What to Do If You're Being Abused 102

Don't Make Excuses for the Abuse 103

Chapter 11. A Match Made in Hell: Narcissists And Empaths 106

What is an Empath? 106

Why Are Narcissists And Empaths Drawn to Each Other? 109

Is There a Future For This Relationship? 111

How an Empath Can be Severely Emotionally Damaged by a Narcissist 112

Points to Take From This Chapter 114

Chapter 12 – How to stop being manipulated by a deceiver 116

   Clarify yourself 116

   Do some ground exercise 117

   Decide whether you want to continue the relationship 118

   Reach out to a trusted loved one or friend 119

   Take a Stand 119

Dealing with the Narcissist 120
  Take a step back and analyze the situation. 120
  Accept that the narcissist will not change. 121
  Seek help. 121
  Set boundaries. 121
  Be realistic. 122
  Remember that your value as a person does not depend on the narcissist. 122
  Speak to them in a way that will make them aware of how they will benefit. 122
  Find proof of or document any kind of abuse. ... 123
  Do not fall for the narcissist's tactics again. 123
  Leave. 123

Chapter 13- Narcissistic Personality Disorder 124
  Symptoms and characteristics of narcissistic personality disorder 125
  Narcissistic personality disorder: causes 126
  Narcissistic personality disorder: treatment 127
  Criteria for Narcissistic Personality Disorder 130
  Characteristics of narcissistic personality disorder 134

Chapter 14- Toxic Relationships Recovery 139
  How to Reduce Conflicts in Relationships 139
    Forgiveness 140

- Invest in Yourself 141
- Experiment with other methods. 143
- Find an Outlet 143
- Research 144
- Exercise 145
- Challenge Your Comfort Zone 146
- Self-soothing 147
- Praise Yourself 147
- Stop the Comparison 148
- Time for Yourself 149
- Therapy 149

How to Know When it's Time to Go 152

Conclusion 155

Introduction

Gaslighting occurs in personal relationships and professional relationships, and in other cases, gaslighting is used by public figures to change the perceptions of targeted members of the population. Gaslighting is a form of psychological abuse. It can make you start to doubt your ability to perceive reality correctly. It can make you think you didn't see what you thought you saw or hear what you thought you heard; and you start to wonder if you can trust the information you are getting from your five senses. Moreover, this, in turn, will make you begin to think that there must be something wrong with you, and you will begin to doubt your sanity.

It doesn't matter whether it is happening in a personal relationship (parent to child, between romantic partners) or a professional relationship at work or even between members of the same community. Gaslighting creates an abusive situation which can cause serious health problems if the victim continues to be in such a position for a long time.

And no matter whether it occurs in a personal relationship or a working relationship, between a public figure and the members of the public or somewhere else, it is essential to be aware of the signs that you or someone you know might be a victim of gaslighting, as this awareness is the first step to getting out of the damaging situation. The first step to take towards being free from gaslighting is to recognize exactly what gaslighting is. It is often very hard to recognize the signs of gaslighting, because they affect the mind so much that, after a long period of time, the victim doesn't trust their own thoughts.

This book discusses in detail how to distinguish gaslighting behavior from typical behavior by shedding light on the different kinds of gaslighting techniques. It also aims to provide you with information about what to do if you find yourself a victim of such a negative situation.

Gaslighting, which will be defined fully in the following chapters, is a technique used by narcissists to manipulate people. Narcissists are self- centered and arrogant people who lack empathy for others. They live in their own world and believe they are unique and special. Hence, they always seek attention and praise from others.

A narcissist will frequently use gaslighting, as a narcissist's goal is to disorient the victim to gain total control over them. A narcissist achieves this aim by gradually sowing seeds of doubt in the victim's mind, and in the end, the narcissist controls the victim to do their bidding.

In addition to promoting awareness about gaslighting, this book is written with the more precise aim of exposing the extent to which narcissists use gaslighting as a means of manipulation to control and abuse their victims both physically and mentally. They expose the words narcissists say and the actions they take to abuse victims. It is one thing to recognize what gaslighting is, and it is another to know how narcissists use it. It is also a different thing entirely to uncover the effects of gaslighting and guard against them - or better still, avoid the effects in the first place.

Most importantly, they show you how to protect yourself and even remove yourself from the control of a gaslighting narcissist.

Chapter 1. Gaslighting

Gas-lighting is the endeavor of someone else to wind your reality. Narcissists can't and don't assume liability for their conduct. Rather, they look to disgrace and accuse others of evading the awful feelings. This is once in a while referred to as projection.

The problem is, gaslighting is slippery. It plays on our most exceedingly awful feelings of dread, our most restless musings, and our most profound wishes to be comprehended, acknowledged, and loved. At the point when somebody we trust, regard, or love talks with incredible conviction—especially if there's a trace of legitimacy in his words, or if he's hit on one of our "red buttons"—it tends to be difficult not to trust him. Furthermore, when we glorify the deceiver—when we need to consider him to be the love of our life, a commendable boss, or a brilliant parent—then, we make it more difficult to adhere to our sense of reality. Our deceiver should be correct; we have to win his endorsement; thus, the gaslighting goes on. Neither of you might know about what's truly occurring. The gaslighter may truly accept each word he lets you know or genuinely feel that he's just sparing you from yourself. Keep in mind: His own needs are driving him. Your deceiver may appear to be a solid, influential man, or he may have all the earmarks of being an unreliable, fit of rage tossing young man; in any case, he feels frail and feeble. To feel groundbreaking and safe, he needs to demonstrate that he is correct, and he needs to get you to concur with him. Then, you have admired your deceiver and are edgy for his endorsement, although you may not intentionally understand this. But if there's even a little bit of you that believes you're bad enough without anyone else—if even a little piece of you believes you need your gaslighter's love or endorsement to be fulfilled—at that point, you are powerless to gaslight. What's more, a deceiver will exploit that helplessness to make you question yourself, again and again.

Gaslighting defies boundaries

When somebody is gaslighting you, they are trying to convince you that your boundaries and perceptions are ridiculous and invalid.

If something they say bothers you because it is abusive or untrue, they will tell you that you are overreacting, or that what you are saying is stupid. They will tell you that it doesn't bother anybody else except you and that you're just being overly sensitive. Even spiritual people are not immune from this, because you might be told that their behavior wouldn't bother you if you were more enlightened. So, in essence, gaslighting and manipulation techniques make you doubt your boundaries or make you drop your boundaries altogether by convincing you that your boundaries are stupid and invalid.

The truth is that your boundaries aren't anybody's business but yours. Nobody gets to determine what boundaries you will have. If something bothers you, then nobody gets to tell you how you feel. When you enforce a boundary, you are not only fighting for the boundary itself, but, more importantly, for your right to set boundaries in the first place. Don't let another person convince you that your boundary isn't big enough for you to take a stand over. It is. Such a way of thinking is really disrespectful.

It's very disrespectful and dishonoring to stand on somebody else's boundary. There is a difference between controlling somebody else by telling them how to behave, and setting a boundary by which you are telling the person not to behave a certain way to you. Reinforcing a boundary means that you are going to have to walk away from someone or from something when they do something wrong to you. Now, realize that it's not about stopping someone from living their life the way they want to live their life, nor is it taking their freedom away from them. It's simply about choosing to engage with or not engage with people who behave in a certain way or who don't respect your boundaries.

Setting up an angry beast

The second form of manipulation is to become an angry beast. This is where somebody tries to become angrier than you when you get angry with them, in order to squash your challenge or rebellion. You might even be just mildly annoyed about something and want to talk to your partner about it, but they explode at you so that you find yourself backing down. You will be so shocked because you were talking about something which was relatively small, and they just turned it into something huge. You will want to back down and not deal with that type of drama. Often, you will be trying to defend your boundaries, and that is what causes the explosion.

This angry beast will come at you with an emotional response that is way out of proportion to the situation or the position that you're trying to defend. You will back down and, often times, you won't even try to stand up for yourself again because you are absolutely not willing to go up against that angry beast. The deceiver is counting on that.

But when you are defending a proper boundary or setting a boundary, it doesn't really matter what the boundary is all about nor does it really matter whether that person sees it as valid or not. Once you have clearly communicated a boundary and the other person says that he will not accept it, you must follow through on the consequences or you will be intimidated into silence and submission. That is what the angry beast wants.

Hijacking the issue

The next manipulative technique is hijacking the issue. This happens when you raise a topic that challenges someone, and he takes it off on a tangent to distract you so that you will not set that boundary or defend that boundary. For example, let's say it's late at night and your spouse hasn't come home from work. They haven't called and you are really worried because you have no idea where they are or if something has happened to them. They finally come home, and you confront them with how worried you were, and ask them where they were and why they didn't even call you to let you know that they would be late.

Rather than answer your concern and questions, they go off on a tangent about how stressed they are at work and how you're not just getting it. They might start to get angry and accuse you of having no sympathy for them. You then find yourself on the defensive side of the conversation, and even apologize to them. Now you're no longer talking about the original topic – how late they were and why they didn't call – but talking about them, and what's bothering them. In the end, they will avoid answering your question altogether.

They have hijacked the conversation and turned it in a different direction. You will often find yourself sitting them down and apologizing to them, and feeling like you shouldn't bother them with your little concerns.

People who use these manipulation tactics are not doing so in a conscious way. They're not doing this on purpose. So they are not hijacking a conversation on purpose, but they are doing it none the less. They don't intend to work up to being an angry beast, or trample on your boundaries, but they do. They do it to control and manipulate you into always putting them first.

Chapter 2. Understanding the Ins and Outs of Gaslighting

In 1944, a movie called **Gaslight** was released that changed the way people thought about manipulation and its immense power. This movie shows the story of a husband character that manipulates his wife and her life to such an extent that she begins to believe that she has become insane.

In this movie too, just like in my life, the wife, Paula, gets completely caught up with the charms of Gregory, the man who woos and wins her. After a whirlwind romance, they get married, and then the tragedy begins. Gregory begins to show his true personality so subtly that Paula begins to think that everything is alright with her husband and that she is going crazy.

The husband in the film dimmed the gas lights in the house and insisted that the wife imagined that the light was dim. His insistence and manipulation were so powerful that the poor, hapless woman begins to think that she is going crazy. And so, the name gaslighting came to be used for such devious and evil manipulative tactics to deliberately steer people away from their real lives and life experiences.

The movie itself is based on a 1938 play of the same name. The ultimate aim of the villainous husband was, of course, to drive his wife to insanity so that he could put her away in a mental institution and claim her inheritance.

Gaslighting is the name used by psychologists to refer to the tactics used by people with a personality disorder to control and manipulate the lives of other people, either individuals or a group of people. These tactics are so strong and go so deep that the manipulated people tend to doubt and question everything in their own lives; their reality, perceptions, feelings, experiences, and interpretations of these experiences. If someone can have this kind of maniacal control over your life, then there is little doubt that your life and sanity are in danger.

At this juncture, it is important to differentiate gaslighting from those tactics that many people use to annoy and irritate the people around them. Gaslighting tactics have a dark quality that annoying but innocuous behavior of certain people doesn't have. It is imperative that you clearly differentiate between the two so that you don't end up judging everyone you come across wrongly.

But you must know for certain that gaslighting is a very serious problem, and you must learn to discern such behavior and stay as far away from such people as possible. After all, having your reality taken from you can be quite dangerous, and if not managed sensibly can prove disastrous for you and your loved ones.

The difficult thing about understanding gaslighting is that the behavioral signs might start out as something very small and insignificant. For example, the manipulator could correct a small detail in a story or life experience you are narrating. Of course, then his or her correction makes sense, and you accept it wholeheartedly. Slowly, that 'past victory' becomes the focal point and keeps rearing its ugly head in all your interactions with the concerned individual, and before you know it, you become his or her slave completely losing touch with your reality and life.

Deliberately, you will be pushed to such an extent that taking simple daily decisions might become difficult for you. Driven by the seeds of self-doubt sowed by the deceiver, you could find yourself second-guessing every decision you make. Like I already told you in the introduction chapter, even the clothes I wore became my husband's decision. At some point, the victim is likely to feel that he or she cannot take any decision whatsoever and depends on every little thing on the manipulator.

Furthermore, the aggressor will slowly convince you that his or her behavior is also your fault. The more you apologize for your behavior, the greedier the aggressor's ego becomes, and the person demands an increasing level of apology and supplicating behavior from you.

The aggressor gets so deep into his or her gaslighting attitude that you will find it exceedingly difficult to reach out and seek help from other people in the fear that they will go against your aggressor. When you are completely and irrevocably under the aggressor's control, then the person dumps you and seeks new 'conquests.'

History of Gaslighting

While the term 'gaslighting' was introduced during the early 1940s, the concept of manipulative behavior for controlling people and altering people's imagined realties has been part of human history for a long time. The victims were simply 'diagnosed' with this condition. They simply withered away in a lunatic asylum or some other institution, alone, depressed, and completely neglected.

Can you recall the story of 'The Emperor Clothes?' What happened there? Did the smart salesman drive every observer on the street to believe that the emperor was clothed in the finest of garments when, in reality, he was stark naked? A little, guileless child saved the day for the rest of the people who believed that if they couldn't see the clothes on their emperor, then it was their fault.

In 1981, psychologist Edward Weinshel wrote an article entitled "Some Clinical Consequences of Introjection: Gaslighting," in which he explained the concept in the following way. The manipulator 'externalizes and projects' the image or thought, and the victim 'internalizes and assimilates' the information into his or her psyche unquestioningly. The 'victim' takes in all the faults, mistakes, and irrationality in such relationships.

Why Does Gaslighting Happen?

Simply put, gaslighting is all about having control. This need for control or domination could stem from personality disorders like narcissism, antisocial issues, unresolved childhood trauma, or any other reason.

Gaslighting behavior is usually seen between people involved in power dynamics where one person invariably wields more power than the other person or people in the relationship equation. The victim of gaslighting tactics is typically on a lower rung than the manipulator and is also terrified of losing something in the relationship. The target of the manipulative relationship is likely to be a codependent partner in the relationship.

For example, in a romantic relationship, the wife might feel the compulsion to put up with manipulative behavior because she WANTS to be in the relationship and/or desires the other things that it brings. Such people are ready to change their perceptions to align with those of the manipulative partner so as to avoid conflicts and to allow things to happen smoothly.

On the other hand, the manipulator continues to be one because he or she is scared of being seen as something less important or significant than desired. Another critical perspective of the deceiver is that the person may not realize that he or she is behaving in ways that could harm or hurt the 'target.' They could be indulging in gaslighting tactics simply because they were reared like that.

For example, if a person was brought up by parents who believe in the concept of absolute certainty, then this person may not know that other perspectives can exist and that they can be right. Such people could be primed to think that anyone who has a different approach or perspective is wrong. Further, they could believe that people with these 'wrong' notions should be corrected, and thus resort to gaslighting tactics; an approach found commonly in a family and among loved ones.

And then, there are the ones who employ gaslighting to show off their dominance and power with little or no care toward the pain and agony inflicted on the target. Sometimes, the 'dominance and power' could also be a facade for the manipulator's insecurities and fears. Whatever it is, gaslighting is employed to dominate unfairly over other people.

Where Does Gaslighting Happen?

Gaslighting can happen and be experienced by anyone and everyone. For example, you could be a victim of such tactics from your spouse, partner, colleague, or sometimes, even a parent. In fact, gaslighting tactics are not restricted to the personal or professional realm.

Gaslighting strategies are used even in public life, affecting an entire group of people. There are multiple instances in which you can clearly see gaslighting techniques by President Donald Trump and his administration. Most experts agree that politics is a field where spreading lies is taken and accepted to be a stereotypical attitude. However, President Trump seems to have taken it a bit too far.

In the initial days of his office, President Trump - along with his administration staff - are believed to have lied so blatantly that there was a shade of arrogance and utter contempt for the intelligence of the American people. It was like the concerned officials were baiting the common people, telling them to rise up and revolt against the nastiness if you can; this was a clear sign of narcissistic personality disorder.

For instance, the administration lied about the crowd size at the Presidential swearing-in. It was clear that photos from President Obama's swearing-in were manipulated to look like the current one. It was so easy to detect this lie that for some people, it was like a war cry to the media, which was most likely to be discredited by Americans for putting such lies on their websites and publications.

At a personal level, gaslighting tactics are used by manipulative people who want to control the lives of their family members. Think of a physically and emotionally abusive spouse wreaking havoc on his or her partner or the children in the family, and you can easily discern gaslighting behavior.

Where is Gaslighting Typically Seen?

Geographically speaking, gaslighting behavior is not exclusive to any part of the world. Wherever power dynamics are in play and where the need and desire for control over people and resources exist, gaslighting behavior can be witnessed. Multiple studies reveal that this kind of unpleasant and dangerous behavior is prevalent not only in personal relationships but also at the workplace, and even in public life as in the way some politicians and their coterie interact with the common man on the street.

MHR, an HR services provider, conducted a survey in the UK which revealed some shocking numbers. Over 3000 people undertook the survey, and 58% of this group claimed that they had experienced what they believed was gas-lighting behavior at their workplace. About 30% said they did not experience such behavior while 12% said that they didn't know! The disturbing results of this survey poll reveal how widespread gaslighting is in the UK. Some examples of gaslighting behaviors at the workplace include:

- Taking credit for your work

- Mocking you, your behavior or dress style in front of other colleagues

- Setting unreasonable and unrealistic deadlines

- Deliberately withholding information that is crucial for the success of a project you are working on

Most of the elements mentioned above are seemingly insignificant but add up to a lot in retrospect. And moreover, unlike bullying, which is easily discernible, gaslighting behaviors are subtle and are meant to slowly but surely put doubt on your capabilities and value to the organization. Such attitudes cannot be caught until after the damage is done to the target's psyche.

Another US-based report says that 3 out of 4 people in the country are not aware of the term, and this state of ignorance is despite the widespread prevalence of gaslighting behavior in the entertainment and media industries where power-play dynamics are perhaps the strongest.

Nearly 75% of the surveyed people said that they had heard of the term but did not know its meaning. The study revealed that about a third of the female population had termed their romantic partners as 'crazy' or 'insane' in a very serious way. About 25% of the male population had also used these two words to describe their partners.

Therefore, gaslighting behavior is not restricted to any particular geography or industry, and can be witnessed in different countries, cultures, and industries.

Common Gaslighting Situations

Here are some common examples of gaslighting scenarios that could help you understand if and when you are being gaslighted by various perpetrators.

In a home environment - Alice's father, Andrew, is a bitter and angry man who is carrying a lot of negativity right from his childhood. His power play is most evident with Alice, thanks to her dependence on him for a lot of things. Alice's mother is the breadwinner in the family and is away most of the time at work.

Alice spent a lot more time with her father than her mother and had unwittingly built herself into a codependency situation with Andrew. She was highly sensitive to his mood swings and was always worried that some action or behavior of hers would bring on a dark mood in her father.

Whenever her father was in a dark mood, he would lash out at Alice by saying that 'You're worthless,' 'I wonder why you were born,' and quite frequently using foul language too. If Alice tried to argue back with him, he would laugh it off and say, 'Why are you so unnecessarily sensitive?'

Alice had become so accustomed to this situation at home that she did not even think it important enough to speak to her mother about it that was too busy with her work to find time for her daughter. Alice was completely under her father's control and even accepted it as natural. She believed that her father was only helping her toward self-improvement and that there was nothing wrong with him.

Another common situation is when adult children manipulate their old parents. Here is a sample case that you are likely to find in many homes.

In a romantic relationship - In the eyes of most people, Julie's life could be seen as being as ideal. Married for over five years to her first love who is now an adoring husband, financially secure (her husband, John, is an investment banker who rakes in the moolah), and with two beautiful children, Julie might look like there is no dearth of happiness in her life. And yet, she knows what she is going through. Before her marriage, Julie was an artist with some great skills.

After she got married, John did his best to prevent his wife from trying to advance her skills and make a name for herself in the art world. He always found fault with her work and made her feel worthless. Every time she tried to paint something, he would say, 'A lousy artist like you is not going to make it in the art world which is filled with brilliant artists. Your work will never match up to theirs. Don't waste time and money on this. Instead, just focus on looking after the family.'

Also, he would always bring up a bad experience that she had had during her early artist days. She had created a painting and wanted feedback from a famous artist who was a good friend of her husband's. The man had said that her skills were way below even an average artist and that she should not even try moving forward. Julie's husband never failed to bring up that comment and used it to make her believe that she was fit for nothing more than taking care of the family.

Julie's husband used that one bad experience and feedback to remind her of her worthlessness continually, and repeated practice and such habitual behavior enslaved her to her husband completely. Now, although she lives comfortably, she realizes that her life is actually empty. She wants to break free from her husband's manipulative ways, but he uses their children to strengthen his power over her.

In a workplace scenario - Jolly was a salesgirl in a large cosmetic showroom. After working for five years, she was given a promotion to work in, which not only gave her a higher salary but also opened up career growth prospects. Jolly was very happy with the promotion and started working with her new boss, Penny.

Initially, Jolly found Penny helpful and sweet. Slowly, Penny started passing on insignificant tasks to Jolly, who did them uncomplainingly. However, this did not stop at all and, in fact, increased so much that she had no time and energy to learn anything new at the job. She was just about able to finish all the work assigned by her boss, who kept her at arm's length and discouraged interactions of all kinds except with giving out tasks.

A department meeting was called one day, and Jolly was part of it. Penny addressed the other people and said, 'Meet Jolly, who has been with us for nearly three months now, and she has yet to learn the ropes of the new department. I hope she catches up soon or else we might have to send her back after demoting her.' Jolly turned red with embarrassment and shame at this open and unexpected insult from her boss. And she realized that she had unwittingly become a victim of gaslighting tactics!

Emotional Hot Spots that are targeted

Nearly anyone can be a target to gaslighting tactics considering the subtlety involved in the process. Very few people can really discern the difference between gaslighting and simple annoying behavior. Most often, people will tend to categorize gaslighting behaviors as a mere annoyance and tend to ignore it. Yet, there are certain types of people who become easy targets for gaslighting. Some of them are:

Empaths - Empaths are people who are extremely sensitive to everything that is happening around them. They can quickly, and most often, unwittingly absorb both positive and negative energies from their environment. Such people can be easy targets for deceivers because it is quite easy to influence them. Just sending negative vibes to empaths can enhance their sensitivity to a deceiver's needs.

Insecure people - Deceivers typically target people with significant inferiority complexes. Men and women who feel insecure about themselves are easy targets considering that they are already in a vulnerable condition.

Moreover, insecure people are continuously looking for positive affirmation from others, which is exactly what deceivers want in the initial stages of any new relationship. Gaslighting tactics start with heaping praise, often when it is not necessary and praises on the victims initially, and once they are trapped, the true color of deceivers come to the fore.

And yet, it is time to reiterate that some deceivers are so good at what they do that even the sanest and most sensible people can become their targets. Therefore, it makes sense to be aware of the concept of gaslighting tactics and their multiple negative effects and to be wary of such people.

Chapter 3. How to spot a gaslighter

If there is an attribute that deceivers appear to have in abundance, it is charm. They are generally likable people that appear to overflow tons of charm, and this may make it difficult to identify them on the surface. There are, however, a few manners of behavior by which they can be identified, and these include:

Withholding: Here the deceiver retains information on what they know or what is the fact by pretending not to understand their victims. They may begin sentences with phrases like "Are you trying to confound me by?" or "Please, don't accompany this again. Haven't I told you...?" It is a tactic to perplex the victim by making him/her vibe like they are off-base or misconstrued a situation.

Countering: The victim's facts are made to be false as victims are blamed for their 'carelessness' or 'jumbling things up' although the victim's memory is great.

Diverting: In this case, the deceiver attempts to occupy the victim or make them question themselves by changing the subject of discussion. An example is "I'm certain your crazy sister advised you to screen my calls." Or "None of this is valid, you're making them up to hurt me."

Downplaying facts: When the victim complains about an unsavory situation or communicates a fear, the deceiver laughs at the issue or downplays its earnestness, making the victim feel like a youngster with a tantrum. You hear phrases like "You're angry because of that?"

Outright denial: The deceiver will deny guarantees that they made, totally telling the victim that they never said so and that the whole conversation happened in the victim's mind. For example, "I never advised you to keep dinner waiting for me!"

Pathologizing: Especially savage deceivers may choose to play specialist with your mental health and 'diagnose' you of instability in an offer to conceal their behavior. They can proceed to make claims that you are 'unstable,' 'not all there,' 'spacey,' or 'vengeful' in an offer to unhinge their victims. They may even advise you to book an appointment with a psychiatrist, all the while acting as if they are working for your wellbeing and subsequently making you accept that something is genuinely amiss with you.

Discrediting: A deceiver will, under the pretense of helping you, spread falsehoods and bits of gossip about you to the people within your circle. They would pretend to be stressed over you and utilize that chance to tell others that you are unstable or have been acting bizarre. They may also turn around to reveal to you that others think you are crazy as a way to drive a wedge among you and the people you would normally go to for help.

Put blames on you: A deceiver will always find a way to blame you for whatever off-base they do. Attempt to have an important conversation about how they hurt you, and they will turn the discussion upside down that you will start believing that you are the reason for their bad behavior.

Shaming: Another tool the deceiver utilizes in keeping the victim calm is by unobtrusively shaming them by making victims feel inept about the fact that they have been victimised. You will, at that point, apologize to them for speaking out about a bad behavior you called out when they have convinced you it's all in your head. A husband that has been cheating may turn the tables on you by saying: "I can't trust you would think that I would cheapen our relationship in that manner! If you trust I did this, it means you have been unfaithful to me," he may say.

Use kind words to keep you daydreaming: When you call out a deceiver, they may amaze you by using kind words that may make you assume that maybe they are not all that bad after all. But if they utilize kind words when faced without changing their behavior or stopping the things that hurt you, they are just manipulative because, after some time, you will start thinking that you are excessively emotional.

Chapter 4. Cognitive Dissonance | How Manipulation Affects You

When a person is being manipulated, cognitive dissonance is a common occurrence. You may be asking yourself what cognitive dissonance actually is, and the thought behind it is actually quite simple. When you get a feeling that is uncomfortable because it goes against your beliefs or your normal way of thinking, it is referred to as cognitive dissonance.

A good example of this would be if you are usually an honest person and you tell a lie. Naturally, this is going to make you feel quite uncomfortable. The contradiction of the behavior you expressed as compared to your normal behaviors is quite different, and the person that does this will experience cognitive dissonance.

In general, people try to be consistent with their thoughts, ideas, attitudes, and behaviors. When these items are challenged, or they go against your level of normalcy, many people will try to change this lack of agreement by doing things like overly explaining their behavior or action. This makes it more comfortable and allows them to move past it.

The first theory behind cognitive dissonance came from a psychologist by the name of Leon Festinger. It centered around the fact that most people will do their best to find internal consistency. Festinger said that we all have an internal need to make sure that our behaviors and our belief systems stay consistent. When they are inconsistent, it leads to internal disharmony, which is something everyone will try and avoid if they can. In fact, people will go to great lengths to find internal balance after experiencing cognitive dissonance.

There are a variety of different factors that will impact the amount of dissonance that a person may experience. One of those factors is how concrete they feel in certain beliefs that they hold. Another factor is how consistent they are in their beliefs throughout the course of time. Thoughts and mental actions that are very personal, such as your understanding and belief in yourself can cause greater dissonance inside of you than other beliefs.

The higher value something holds in you internally, the greater the dissonance you will experience if you go against that belief. It is normal for people to have thoughts that clash; however, this is something that tends to come and go as most people strive to have consistent thought patterns, behaviors, and beliefs. The more dissonance a person experiences, the more pressure they will also experience to find balance and relieve themselves of uncomfortable feelings.

It's actually pretty amazing how cognitive dissonance can influence a person's actions, thoughts, and behaviors. Cognitive dissonance can be seen in just about every area of life. It is predominant in situations that behaviors conflict with a person's belief system. This is especially true when dealing with the area of self-identity. Let's look at an example of cognitive dissonance so that you have a very clear understanding of what we are talking about here.

- We see cognitive dissonance occur frequently when people are making purchasing decisions. Let's say you are someone that is very conscious of the environment, and you do your very best to make green decisions. One day you go and buy a new car to find out that it is not very eco-friendly. This will cause cognitive dissonance because you care about being friendly to the environment, yet you are driving a car that is not very

> friendly to the environment. The dissonance can be reduced the number of ways to make the belief and the behavior go together better. You could choose to sell your new vehicle and get one that is going to get better mileage and be friendlier to the environment, or you could choose to cut down on how much you are driving the new car. Some may choose to utilize public transportation or even ride a bike to work. Each one of these is a solution to help resolve the dissonance that is being experienced. They all help bring balance.

There are a variety of ways that people will try to find balance when experiencing dissonance. Minimizing the drawbacks of a decision or action is one way that people do this. A great example is to think about people who smoke, and they may take the time to convince themselves that the risks are being blown out of proportion. This helps their minds to accept the bad habit of smoking and, in turn, alleviate the dissonance hey experience when they smoke and think about it being bad for their health.

Another thing that people will do to get rid of the uncomfortable feelings caused by cognitive dissonance is to look at the beliefs that outweigh the action that was dissonant. This is done by looking for new information to change their old patterns of thinking.

This new information, even if it isn't exactly correct, can allow the uncomfortable feelings to dissipate, leaving the person feeling more balanced and at ease.

People will also try to reduce the significance of the belief that conflicts how they normally feel. An example of this is the person who works in an office building and sits in front of a computer all day. They know that sitting for long periods of time is unhealthy, but it is hard to change it since it is there job to sit in front of that computer. Rather than change their behavior, they will try and justify the action of sitting all day. They do this by telling themselves that the fact that they eat healthily and exercise once in a while will be enough to combat the negative effects of sitting all day. This helps to reduce the uncomfortable dissonance they are experiencing.

The last way that people deal with cognitive dissonance is to change the conflict that is occurring inside. By changing a belief so that it coincides with other beliefs, the dissonance will be alleviated. This change of belief systems is effective when trying to deal with dissonance, but it is also quite difficult. Obviously, if you are trying to change your core values and beliefs to deal with dissonance, it is going to be a challenge.

More often than not, people will find other ways to deal with the cognitive dissonance that does not require them to restructure their entire thought process and beliefs on a particular subject.

It is important to remember that cognitive dissonance can be very disconcerting. When your beliefs and your actions don't match up, it can take a toll on your ability to make decisions that will be beneficial to you. When we notice cognitive dissonance, it should be looked at as an opportunity to grow and learn.

When you are dealing with a gaslighting narcissist, cognitive dissonance can give you a great clue as to what is going on. If you find yourself doing, saying, or agreeing with things that go against your values and beliefs because of what someone else is saying, it is a good sign that you are being manipulated. Our bodies do a great job of helping us understand the experiences that unfold in front of us on a daily basis. You can use cognitive dissonance to your advantage so that you maintain the beliefs and values that ring true to you rather than allow yourself to be influenced by a nefarious manipulator.

Effects of Manipulation

Manipulation can come in a variety of different forms, and unfortunately, there are a variety of different negative effects that come along with it. Whether you are mentally or emotionally manipulated, the effects can be devastating. Sometimes they are short term effects that can be moved passed relatively easily while other times they are long-lasting and can impact your life forever. When you know the effects of manipulation, you are better equipped to handle them, and your life will be able to improve more easily.

Psychological and emotional abuse occurs when people are manipulated, and unfortunately, they are not simple wounds that will heal. In fact, it is likely if you have been abused with manipulation that you will carry the scars for the rest of your life. Seeking help is sometimes the best course of action, depending on the experience that you have had. When it comes to mental manipulation, you may find that you have problems with trust, security, respect, and intimacy, and these are only a few of the issues that you may be facing.

We are going to take the time to look at the short- and long-term effects that occur from mental and emotional manipulation.

The gaslighting tactic, is both mental and emotional abuse. So, if you have or you are dealing with a narcissist who uses gaslighting, it is very likely that you are experiencing some of these effects. Recognizing them can be the first step toward finding improved health and happiness.

The Short-Term Effects of Manipulation:

- If you have been mentally or emotionally manipulated, it can be very difficult to understand what is unfolding. You may feel surprised or confused by events. The feelings of "this can't be so" are very common. You may question why the people closest to you are acting so strange, even if they aren't acting strange at all.

- It is also likely that you will question yourself if you have been through or you are going through this type of abuse. You may wonder if your memory is deceiving you, or you may feel like there is something wrong with you, in general. When everything you do is questioned, this is the result. Gaslighting will cause this effect frequently as you will always be wrong or questioned by the narcissistic party in the relationship.

- If you have experienced mental or emotional manipulation, another short-term effect could be anxiety and hypervigilance. People become vigilant toward themselves and other people to try and avoid further manipulation. They will avoid behaviors that make things chaotic or ones that may end in outbursts. Anxiety will rule them, and any extra chaos could lead to a break down so, they will avoid any and everything that may cause that.

- Passiveness is another effect that comes from being psychologically and emotionally manipulated. Oftentimes, more emotional pain comes when you take action in a mentally or emotionally abusive relationship, so being passive becomes part of everyday life. It is important to note that being passive can be a hard thing to break, especially during times of emotional stress. Being passive can become a default and a constant presence in day to day life.

- The feeling of guilt or shame is also a common effect of mental and emotional manipulation. When you are constantly being blamed for the negative actions taking place in your life, you start to believe that you are the cause. This can lead to feelings of guilt or shame as you take their bad behavior out on yourself. Obviously, this is only going to make you feel worse, and it is an unfortunate side effect of being with a narcissist or a manipulator.

- Avoiding making eye contact with others is another short-term effect of mental and emotional manipulation. When we don't make eye contact with people, it allows us to feel smaller like you can hide inside of yourself and that you will take up less space. This is a common thing to do when someone is hard on you all the time and makes you feel as if you are insane. We feel that it helps to protect us in some sort of way. Fortunately, this is a side effect that tends to go away rather quickly after we remove the toxic manipulator from our lives and start being around people that genuinely care for us in healthy ways.

- The last short-term effect that we would like to mention is the feeling that you need to walk on eggshells around people. When you live your life with an emotional or mental manipulator around, you will never be able to tell what will upset them next. Due to this fact, you will start to obsess about everything that you are doing. The obsession takes place because you are trying to avoid causing any outbursts, and it can bleed over into other relationships that you may have.

While there is nothing good to be said about being manipulated psychologically or emotionally, we can take some solace in the fact that if we can move away from these abusive relationships, the above issues will likely resolve. There are side effects of these types of abuse that will not go away so easily.

In fact, there are side effects of emotional manipulation that could stick around forever. Seeking professional help to figure out a course of action to help you heal is oftentimes the best place to start. Let's take a look at some of the long-term effects that one may experience if they have suffered or are suffering from mental or emotional manipulation.

The Long-Term Effects of Manipulation:

- One of the 1st and most devastating long-term effects of mental manipulation are the feelings of isolation or complete numbness. Many find that they feel they are no longer a participant of the world but that they have become observers. Things that used to make them happy now don't make them feel anything at all. When someone no longer recognizes their emotions, it leads to a sense of hopelessness. Many fear that they will never be able to accurately feel or experience their emotions again. This long-term effect does not have to last forever. If you are able to get out of the abusive relationship, you can find healing for your damaged emotions.

- Another long-term effect is constantly seeking approval. People that have been emotionally or mentally manipulated are likely going to be exceptionally nice to every person they come into contact with. Additionally, they will go to great lengths to please others. They will likely be extremely focused on their appearance, and they will constantly be striving to accomplish more and more goals. They will do their best to be perfect in every way so that others will approve of them. While some of these things don't seem so bad, keep in mind that it will be to an extreme which is not good.

- People that have suffered the abuse of manipulation are oftentimes left with feelings of resentment. This resentment can be seen in different ways like impatience, frustration, irritability, and placing blame. When you have been treated poorly, it can be extremely difficult to witness anything other than that negative behavior. So, releasing feelings of resentment can be quite difficult, especially if you are going at it on your own.

- Depression is another real threat to those that have experienced or are experiencing manipulation. Depression is something that may never be overcome once it has taken a hold on your life. It takes a lot of work to dig your way out of the effects of depression. When people are depressed, they start to lose faith in those that they care about and that care about them. They feel alone and sad without a sense of purpose within their world. It becomes hard for them to believe in themselves or in anyone else, and this takes a lot of time to heal from.

- Another long-term effect that may be experienced is the excessive judgment of yourself and others. Due to the fact that a narcissistic manipulator will constantly judge you, you will start to judge yourself and others much more critically. Here will be very high standards when it comes to things like appearance and behavior. This can lead to problems within all of your relationships, including your relationship with yourself.

As noted, long term effects can be devastating an impact your life negatively in just about every aspect. There is hope in coming back from these negative effects after you have been able to remove yourself from a manipulative situation. Keep in mind that there is nothing wrong with admitting you need help and seeking it out. You really can find a lot of healing through therapy or groups, which will help you become yourself once again, allowing you to truly start enjoying life.

Chapter 5. How Gaslighting Narcissists operate to make their Victim Think that they are Crazy

So, we mentioned that narcissists have a hand in gaslighting, but what do they do/ they actually are huge manipulators, and they play a major role in changing the reality of others. Here, we'll discuss how they gaslight others, and why narcissists are bad news for many people.

What Is A Narcissist?

A narcissist is, by definition, someone that suffers from narcissistic personality disorder. Those who are narcissists tend to have an overly inflated sense of importance, and a need for admiration and attention in their relationships, and oftentimes don't have empathy for others.

Narcissists only care about themselves. They don't worry about you, or the guy next to you, but instead, they're only in it for their own benefit. However, they actually have an incredibly fragile ego that will shatter and is very vulnerable if they're hit with the smallest amount of criticism.

Narcissists are textbook manipulators, and they're not fun to deal with. This type of personality causes many issues in different areas of life, and you may run into one of these types without even realizing it. Typically, though, those who suffer from narcissistic personality disorder are unhappy in a general sense if they're not given the admiration they want. They may find all of their relationships unfulfilling, and others may not like being around these types of people.

So how does a narcissist come into your life? Well, those that suffer from this love to latch onto those that will hype them up, making them feel like they're special or unique, and in turn enhance their own self-esteem as a result. They may desire an immense amount of admiration and attention and have difficulty taking criticism in the slightest. They oftentimes see all criticism as defeat.

They are incredibly envious of your accomplishments, to the point where they will want to undermine them however, they can. This can be anything from snarky accomplishments regarding your success to underhanded comparing of others.

Narcissists love to use gaslighting too, but we'll get to that in a bit. For now, let's talk about how they will undermine you. If you do something great, they'll try to belittle it, saying that it's not worth it, and you need to do better. Sometimes, if the narcissist is a parent, they'll compare you to your sibling or someone else in the family. They oftentimes will try to belittle anything you do, turning you into a mess in response.

It's not good, and narcissists in general only care about themselves. Of course, many times only a small fraction of people are actual narcissists, but in general, there are more male narcissists than female narcissists, and you oftentimes will run into them when you're dealing with bosses, coworkers, or even people you may be friends with or date.

But, how can these people use gaslighting? Well, they do so in a very crafty manner.

Narcissism and Gaslighting

Narcissists love to use gaslighting. In fact, it's their favorite, most preferred tool of gaslighting. Why is that? Well, it's because it's the perfect way to make you think you're crazy, to completely undermine what you think is right, and to basically tell you that your way of thinking is wrong.

Remember, gaslighting is a very sneaky way of making you feel like your reality is so distorted to the point where the person will question their own sanity or even their memory. Their goal is to make it so that they're right, you're wrong, and that's all they want from this.

The goal is to make you think you're crazy, which we'll get to in a bit. There are other tools narcissist will use, but gaslighting is their bread and butter.

"Oh, I never said that."

"Oh, you're remembering it wrong, clearly you should get yourself checked out."

If you've ever heard those two things before from someone, you're dealing with a Grade A Narcissist.

Gaslighting is used by narcissists because it's how they love to hide the abuse they're inflicting upon you. In essence, gaslighting is lying straight to your face, with one singular goal in mind, to be the ones in control, the center of attention, and you're nothing.

Basically, every time a narcissist gaslights you, they're basically completely ruining what sense of reality you have, making you realize that it's nothing, and they're everything.

They want to break you down slowly but surely. Memory is one of the easiest ways to do this. Why is that? Well, it's because they know that if you can't remember things right, you're not going to be able to trust yourself, distorting your own personal perception and reality that comes with this.

So yes, it does happen like that, and the goal is for you to completely rely on the abuser to tell you what's real so that over time the abuser is the one in control of your life, the one taking the reins here in the game.

The Art of Making Others Crazy

This is something that a lot of narcissists use gaslighting for. Remember, gaslighting is basically refuting anyone's reality, making it so that what they think is right really isn't.

When a narcissist gaslights, they will put down and refute anything that you say. They will do this to make it sound like they're the ones who are right when in reality, it's their own mind games.

It's all a game for a narcissist. They want to make it so that your reality isn't correct. While you might believe that you're right, the narcissist will tell you right away that you aren't. Over time as you continue to be refuted by the narcissist, you start to doubt your own reality. You start to think that you're the bad guy when in reality, it's just your narcissist playing games.

When a narcissist gaslights, they can change the view that you have of people, in general, being good. You might think that people, in general, are good, which they are, but oftentimes, if you have a narcissist in your life, this person will not protect your feelings. Someone you may think is good turns out to be bad, and someone that you thought was bad turns out to be good since that's how the narcissist wants you to think.

A narcissist will use gaslighting for the sole reason of, they know exactly how to manipulate you. You start to doubt your own reality, and over time, you start to wonder if maybe you are crazy. After all, after so often, you may wonder if you're not right in the head. But remember, more often than not, narcissists were the cause of this, and they're the reason why you think this way.

Lots of times narcissists will start by buttering you up, making you feel loved and appreciated since that's what they want you to believe. After a while, they will start to, over time, start to treat you like crap. When you call them out on it, they'll start to mask their true feelings, and you'll be seeing a totally different side.

But the reality is, that mask that they put on is, of course, their mask, and the abusive nature that they've had till now is their true form.

They will tell you what you think is what happened isn't what happened, but that's actually how it is. But of course, in the world of the narcissist, they'll only make you believe what they think is right.

Gaslighting basically takes away everything that you think is correct, which then causes you to follow what they think is the way when in reality, they're manipulating you.

You're basically forced to believe that you're crazy, or if you don't think you're crazy, that the abuser is wrong, but you can't stand up for yourself. They will either manipulate you until you believe you're wrong and they are right or drive you to the point of insanity.

Deceivers and narcissists love this. Because they know that, once you discount your own personal beliefs enough, you'll start to really think that you are crazy, and slowly start to believe them.

Making People do What the Narcissist Wants

This is done because most of the time, when you start to discount how a narcissist acts, they will immediately gaslight you, saying that it didn't happen this way.

You notice your narcissist abuser is acting gross and mean, and you notice that for example, they're flirting with other girls. They totally are, and you call them out on it, but they will immediately say that isn't the case, tell you that you're crazy, that you're making stuff up, and basically tell you whatever you saw was wrong.

Deep down, you know what the truth is. That the actions you saw were valid, but over time, this person will continuously tell you that you're crazy, that you didn't really hear or say what was said.

You start to doubt your own reality, and you begin to wonder if you remembered everything right. Perhaps you didn't catch the other person flirting with girls. You start to go silent on it. When in reality, your narcissist was totally doing that, didn't come clean, and now this person is seeing girls, and every time you call them out on that, and their own trust and validity, basically tells you that you're insane, and you're wrong.

You stop fighting the narcissist after a while. You notice that every time you fight them there really is no end to it and the fact that you're constantly told that you're crazy every time you do isn't a good thing for you either. So, what do you do from here?

The answer is most people tend to give in to their abusers.

Instead of doing what they feel is right, which is calling out the abuser and recognizing the toxic traits, you start to do exactly what the abuser wants. Because whenever you're gaslight, you start to feel like you're wrong, and that the narcissist is right. You're pretty much duped into believing that the narcissist is the right person, and you're wrong, making your reality practically nothing.

If you let this continue, you're basically feeding the supply of narcissism that the other person craves. You may start to perceive things wrong, and oftentimes, it gets to the point where you swore it was that way, but maybe your stuff is gone, because the narcissist hides it, and then they claim that you're irresponsible, and not worthy of trust. They will then tell you that you're wrong and crazy, and they'll start to make others think that you're crazy.

They will even pit others against you to isolate others. Oftentimes, they'll try to put you against others, so you drop them, and the only person in your life is the narcissist. They'll make up lies, and you can't really trust anyone but the person who is gaslighting you.

When in reality, the one who is gaslighting you is the last person that you should be trusting!

Deceivers don't really realize just how harmful they are, or maybe they do. They will start to make you question even the most random of strangers. You might start to brush off someone's actions as being harmless, but the gaslighted will call it flirting, and soon, you start to attack anyone who comes at you.

Have you ever seen this? Maybe you've experienced it. Where you will hear about how someone was looking at you the wrong way, you start to grow weary and angry with the other person, and over time, those relationships break down since you think they can't be trusted. When in reality, it's the narcissist who can't be trusted, because they're the one putting you in this direction.

A narcissist will hurt literally everyone in your life, pit you against the friends and family that you have so that you're distracted from what the narcissist is really doing, which is feeding you harmful lies.

It's a messy situation and not something that most of us want to deal with.

So yes, a narcissist will use gaslighting. It's the prime tool of narcissist because they know that they can bend others to the will that they have, making it very easy to manipulate them, and that's why many narcissists will smile at you with a warm, fake smile, and then stab you in the back whenever you turn around, or put your family and friends against you, so the only person you can really rely on, is the narcissist themselves

Chapter 6. The Effects of Gaslighting

Effects of Gaslighting

1. Gaslighting can have catastrophic effects on a person's psychological health; the procedure is gradual, chipping away the person's certainty and self-esteem. They may come to accept they merit the abuse.

2. Gaslighting can also influence a person's social life. The abuser may manipulate them into cutting ties with friends and relatives. The individual might also isolate themselves, believing they are unstable or unlovable.

3. Especially when the person escapes the abusive relationship, the effects of gaslighting can persevere. The person may even now question their discernments and have difficulty making decisions. They are also more reluctant to voice their emotions and feelings, knowing that they are probably going to be invalidated.

4. Gaslighting may lead a person to create mental health concerns. The constant self-uncertainty and disarray can contribute to anxiety. A person's sadness and low self-esteem may lead to despondency. Post-traumatic stress and codependency are common developments.

5. Some survivors may battle to confide in others; they may be on constant guard for additional manipulation. The individual may criticize themselves for not catching the gaslighting earlier. Their refusal to show vulnerability might prompt strain in future relationships.

Recovering from Gaslighting

Gaslighting is a secret form of abuse that blossoms with uncertainty. A person can grow to distrust everything they feel, hear, and recollect. One of the most significant things a survivor can get is validation.

The individuals who have encountered gaslighting may also wish to look for therapy. A therapist is a natural party who can aid in reinforcing one's sense of reality. In therapy, an individual can modify their self-esteem and recover command of their lives. A therapist might also treat any mental health concerns caused by the abuse, for example, PTSD. With time and backing, a person can recoup from gaslighting.

Are You Being Gas lighted?

Gaslighting may not include these experience or feelings, but if you recognize yourself in any of them, give it additional attention.

1. You are constantly re-thinking yourself.

2. You ask yourself, "Am I excessively sensitive?" twelve times each day.

3. You regularly feel confounded and even insane at work.

4. You're continually saying 'sorry' to your mom, father, sweetheart, boss.

5. You wonder now and again if you are a "sufficient" sweetheart/wife/representative/companion/little girl.

6. You can't get why, with so many beneficial things in your life, you aren't more joyful.

7. You purchase garments for yourself, goods for your apartment, or other personal buys in light of your partner, considering what he might want rather than what might cause you to feel incredible.

8. You often rationalize your partner's conduct to loved ones.

9. You end up denying data of loved ones, so you don't need to clarify or rationalize.

10. You realize something is off-base, but you can never fully communicate what it is, even to yourself.

11. You begin lying to maintain a strategic distance from the put-downs and reality turns.

12. You experience difficulty settling on basic decisions.

13. You reconsider before raising blameless subjects of discussion.

14. Before your partner gets back home, you go through a list in your mind to foresee anything you may have fouled up that day.

15. There is a sense that you used to be a different person — increasingly sure, progressively carefree, progressively relaxed.

16. You begin addressing your better half through his secretary so you don't need to reveal to him things you're apprehensive may agitate him.

17. You feel as if you can't do anything right.

18. Your children start attempting to shield you from your partner.

19. You get yourself angry with people you've generally coexisted with previously.

20. You feel sad and dreary.

Gaslighting tends to work in stages

From the start, it might be generally minor—in reality; you may not see it. At the point when your partner blames you for intentionally attempting to undermine you by appearing late to his office party, you attribute it to his nerves or expect you didn't generally mean it or maybe even start to ponder whether you were attempting to undermine him—but then you let it go. Inevitably, however, gaslighting turns into a greater piece of your life, distracting your musings and overpowering your feelings.

Eventually, you're buried in full-scale sorrow, miserable and dismal, unfit even to recollect the person you used to be, with your perspective and your sense of self. You may not continue through every one of the three phases. But for many women, gaslighting goes from terrible to more awful.

Stage 1: Disbelief Stage 1 is portrayed by disbelief; your deceiver says something over the top—"That person who approached us for bearings was extremely simply attempting to get you into bed!"— And you can't exactly accept your ears. You think you've misjudged, or perhaps he has, or possibly he was simply kidding. The comment appears to be so unusual; you may ignore it. Or on the other hand, maybe you attempt to address the blunder but without a ton of energy. Possibly you even get into since a long time ago, included arguments, but you're still quite sure of your perspective. Although you'd like your deceiver's endorsement, you don't yet feel frantic for it.

Stage 2: Defense Stage 2 is set apart by the need to safeguard yourself. You scan for proof to refute your deceiver and contend with him fanatically, frequently in your mind, frantically attempting to win his endorsement.

Stage 3: Depression gaslighting is the most challenging of all: downturn. Now, you are effectively attempting to demonstrate that your deceiver is correct, because then perhaps you could do things his way and at long last win his endorsement.

Chapter 7. Signs you are Being Manipulated with Gaslighting

The signs of gaslighting can be hard to see, especially for the person that is being manipulated by this tactic. Obviously, the effects of gaslighting are extremely detrimental. So, if you can recognize the signs of it as it is happening, it gives you an advantage and the possibility of getting out of this toxic situation before it completely destroys you and your life.

Oftentimes, people that care about you will recognize the signs before you will be able to. They may try and talk to you about the issues that they are seeing, but you may not be willing to hear them if the effects of gaslighting have already taken hold.

When someone you trust or once felt that you could trust comes to you and expresses their concern over signs of gaslighting, you should spend time reflecting on what they have to say to ensure that you are not a victim of this horrific abuse.

We are going to discuss a variety of different signs that you may witness if you are being gaslighted. Becoming a victim of gaslighting can impact your life negatively in every way. By looking over the following signs, it may become easier to understand what is going on, which can, in turn, give you the clarity and confidence to remove yourself from your current situation.

If you find yourself doubting your own emotions, you may be experiencing the repercussion of gaslighting. Oftentimes people will try to convince themselves that things really aren't so bad. They will assume they are simply too sensitive and that what they are seeing as reality is tragically skewed from actual reality. If you have never had an issue with doubting your feelings, it can be a very good sign of gaslighting tactics.

Alongside doubting, your emotions will come doubting your perceptions of the events that unfold in front of you, as well as doubting your own personal judgment.

Many people that are being manipulated by gaslighting will be afraid to stand up for themselves and express their emotions. This is due to the fact that when they do the gaslighting narcissist makes them feel bad or inferior for doing so. If you find that you are choosing silence over communication, it is a pretty good sign that gaslighting is present in your relationship.

At one point or another, we will all feel vulnerable or insecure. These are normal feelings; however, if you are in a situation of gaslighting, you will feel this way consistently. You may always feel like you need to tiptoe around your partner, family member, or friend to ensure that they don't have a negative outburst. Additionally, you will start to believe that you are the one causing problems for them instead of the reverse.

The gaslighting narcissist will do their best to sever ties between you and the people that you care about. This can leave the victim feeling powerless and completely alone. The narcissist will convince their victim that the people around them don't actually care. In fact, they will try to convince the victim that everyone thinks that they are crazy, unstable, or flat out insane. These kinds of comments make the victim feel trapped. It also causes them to distance themselves from the people that do actually care, which, intern, makes them in even less control than before.

Another sign that you are in the grips of the abuse that comes from a narcissistic deceiver is feeling that you are crazy or stupid. The narcissist will use a variety of different words and phrases to make you question your own value. This can become extreme to the point that the victim may start repeating these derogatory comments. The sooner you can see the sign of verbal abuse, the sooner you will be able to make the decision to not let it deconstruct your sense of self-worth.

The gaslighting narcissist will do their best to change your perception of yourself. Let's say that you have always thought of yourself as a strong and assertive person, yet all of a sudden, you realize that your behaviors are passive and weak. This extreme change of behavior is a good sign that you are succumbing to gaslighting tactics. When you are grounded in who you really are and what your belief system stands for, it will be harder for the narcissistic deceiver to get you to be disappointed in yourself. When you can recognize that the viewpoint of your worth has changed, it can give you the motivation to take back control of your own life.

Confusion is one of the narcissistic deceiver's favorite tools. They will say one thing one day and then do something completely opposite the following day. The result of these types of actions is extreme confusion.

The behaviors of a narcissistic deceiver will never be consistent. They will always try to keep you on your toes so that you are in a constant state of anxious confusion. This gives them more control. Finding that your partner, family member, or friend is exceptionally inconsistent with their behaviors should clue you in to the fact that you are likely in a toxic relationship with them.

If your friend, partner, or family member teases you or puts you down in a hurtful way too, then minimalize the fact that your feelings are hurt. It is a surefire sign of gaslighting. By telling you that you are too sensitive or that you need to learn how to take a joke, they are brushing your hurt feelings to the side. Someone who truly cares about you, even if teasing, will take the time to acknowledge the fact that they hurt your feelings. If you are constantly being questioned about how sensitive you are, be aware you could be succumbing to the abuse of gaslighting.

Another sign that narcissistic gaslighting is occurring is when you constantly feel that something awful is about to happen. This sense of impending doom starts to manifest early on in gaslighting situations. Many people don't understand why they feel threatened whenever they are around a certain person, but after further investigation and getting away from the narcissist, they understand it completely.

Gut feelings should always be listened to, so if your body is telling you that something is not right between you and another person, you should remove yourself from the situation before things get terribly out of control.

There are always times in our lives that we owe other people apologies; however, when you are in a gaslighting situation, you will spend a plethora of time apologizing to people. You will feel the need to say I'm sorry regardless of if you have done anything wrong or not. You may really be apologizing for simply being there. When we question who we are and our value. It leads us to apologize profusely. If you notice how much you are saying, I'm sorry is increasing, and the things you are saying sorry for are minimal; you may be in a gaslighting situation.

Second-guessing yourself or constant feelings of inadequacy when you are with your narcissistic partner, family member, or a friend are excellent signs that they are gaslighting you. If no matter what you do, it is never good enough, you should be aware that you may be being manipulated.

When it comes to 2nd guessing yourself, we're not just talking about second-guessing your decisions but second-guessing things like your memories.

You may wonder if you are actually remembering things as they happened because your narcissistic abuser constantly tells you differently. If you have never had a problem recreating and discussing your memories and all of a sudden you are trying to figure out whether or not what you are saying is true you may want to take a closer look at the person you are dealing with instead of looking at yourself.

Another sign that you are succumbing to the powers of gaslighting is functioning under the assumption that everyone you come into contact with is disappointed in you in one way or another. Constant feelings that you are messing things up are daunting and unrealistic; however, it is amazing how many people don't recognize when this is happening. They simply start to apologize for all of the time and assume that no matter what they do, they will make a mess of things, which will lead to others being disappointed in them.

When someone that you are in close contact with makes you feel as if there is something wrong with you, it could also be a sign of gaslighting. We aren't talking about physical ailments; we are talking about feeling as if you have fundamental issues. You may sit and contemplate your sanity and reality. Unless these were problems for you prior to entering into a new relationship, you should definitely pay attention to the sign.

Gaslighting can also make it extremely difficult for you to make decisions. Where you once made solid choices for yourself, you now have a sense of distrust in your judgment. This can make decision making extremely difficult. Instead of making your own choices, many victims will allow their narcissistic abusers to make their decisions for them. The other alternative is not making any decisions at all. Obviously, this could have extremely negative impacts on a person's life.

One other great sign that you may be dealing with a gaslighting situation is when someone you are close to constantly reminds you of your flaws. Sure, a bit of constructive criticism is welcomed in most people's lives; however, when your weaknesses or shortcomings are constantly being pointed out by someone that is supposed to care about you, it is a clear sign that something is wrong. You should never despise who you are because of heinous comments made by a narcissist. So, if you take a step back and look at the people in your life, it will be easy to figure out who genuinely cares about you and who is trying to control you based on the way that they speak to you.

Along the same line, where a deceiver will tear you down, they will almost never admit or recognize their own flaws. If their flaws are pointed out, it is likely that they will become aggressive.

The deceiver is almost always on the offensive and ready to attack. This means that they will have an inability to recognize their own inadequacies and they will quickly place the blame on you if you try and point them out. They are excellent at playing the victim. Additionally, misdirection will be used so that they can turn things around and continue to dote on your shortcomings even if they are fictitious.

Another sign that you are being manipulated by a deceiver is when you start to make excuses for their bad behavior. People will go to great lengths to cover up the abuse that they are facing and dealing with on a daily basis. They tell themselves and everyone else that things are OK or even better than OK. The victim will come up with a variety of excuses as to why their narcissistic counterpart is acting the way that they are. These excuses are not usually accepted by the people questioning the victim; however, the victim will just continue to make excuses rather than admit there is an actual problem.

Recognizing these signs can be a bit difficult when you are involved in a gaslighting situation. When these signs are being pointed out to you by friends, relatives, or other people that care about you, take a moment to stop and really think about what they are saying. Accepting the signs of gaslighting abuse can be difficult, but it is also necessary for preserving your happiness and sense of self-worth.

It is important to note that the longer you are in a relationship with a gaslighting narcissist, the harder it will be to recognize the signs. Spending the time at the beginning of a friendship or a relationship to truly get to know the person and decide whether or not continuing on with them will lead to toxicity can save you from devastating abuse. Remember that people are not always what they seem, so being mindful and present in each moment as it occurs is imperative to keeping yourself safe.

Chapter 8. Things Narcissists Say During Gaslighting.

Stuff Your Gaslighting Abuser Says

If there's one thing I've learned from interacting with people who have had to battle being with a manipulative deceiver, it's that without fail, the abusers all seem to have certain choice phrases that they all use. It's almost like they all graduated from Gaslight University or something. Here's what your abuser will say:

1. You're only acting this way because you're so insecure.

2. You're too sensitive!

3. Stop being paranoid.

4. it's really not a big deal.

5. I was only kidding!

6. You take things too seriously.

7. You're acting crazy right now.

8. You know you are a little nuts, right?

9. You're just making all that up.

10. Stop being so hysterical!

11. Can you be any more dramatic?

12. You're so ungrateful!

13. That's all in your head.

14. No, that never happened.

15. You're lying. No one believes you. I'm not buying your nonsense.

16. If you had just paid attention.

17. We've already talked about this. Don't you remember?

18. Don't you think you're maybe overreacting?

19. If you had just listened.

20. You keep jumping to the wrong conclusions.

21. You're the only person I've ever had all these issues with.

22. I'm discussing, not arguing.

23. I know exactly what you're thinking.

24. What does it say about you that that's what you think?

25. The only reason I criticize you is that I'm looking out for you.

26. Don't take every single word I say so seriously.

27. You need to get better at communicating.

28. Calm down.

29. You're overthinking this. It's really not that deep.

30. What if you're wrong again, just like the last time?

Think about the context in which you hear these phrases being said to you. Were you talking about sex? Family? Money? Habits one or both of you have? You'll notice that these phrases often pop up when the conversation is centered upon that.

It's a sad truth that, for the most part, the victim is a woman, and a gaslighting narcissist is a man. The reason for this polarization of genders in narcissism is that, often, women have learned to doubt themselves and to apologize whenever there's a problem or disagreement with their significant others. Men, however, are not socialized this way.

Chapter 9. Empowering Ways to Disarm a Narcissist and Take Control

Techniques to handle narcissists

Now comes the difficult part. Deciding what to do with the narcissistic person in your life, and what the best outcome is. This can depend greatly on your individual circumstances as well as the person at hand.

Get away

Typically, extreme narcissists lack normal levels of empathy, don't pull their own weight, and tend to make the people close to them miserable within the space of a few weeks or months. They are unlikely to have a great deal of insight into their damaging behaviors and are unlikely to have an epiphany compelling them to change.

It may be tempting to try and open their eyes to the cause of their problems, help or change them, but this is far more likely to misfire with defensiveness or lead to resentment (depending on how extreme they are).

Relationships you could potentially cut off include not only romantic partners, friends and ex-colleagues, but also family. If you are not legally bound to remain in contact with someone – such as engaged in a business, joint ownership of property, administration of a will, or where a dependent is involved, then you have the potential to cut away if you need to.

Less drastic steps include taking a break or managing the situation. Breaks can help to gain clarity, but it depends upon the relationship at hand, and whether you deem it to be worth saving. If abuse is currently involved in the relationship, an immediate cut-off should be instigated, rather than attempting to make the best of it.

It's important to choose the people you spend time with wisely, because humans tend to adopt the characteristics of those around them. Professor Nicholas Christakis of Yale University explains this in terms of the ripple effect, whereby altruism and meanness ripple through the networks of people, and become magnified. Whatever enters your system - including the actions of your peers, colleagues and family - will affect your personality development and outlook. Surrounding yourself with good people will make you behave in more kind and empathic ways.

Avoid the inner circle

If you need or want to keep a narcissist in your life, it is much safer to do so at a distance, rather than as part of their inner circle - who become privy to their chaotic changes in temperament. Creating justifiable distance (but remaining warm) allows you to be a welcome part of their life without suffering so many falls from grace. They may well start to think of you quite fondly. Get too close, however, and you may become an undervalued part of the furniture, without your own identity or boundaries to respect. In addition, you are giving more opportunities for your words and actions to be misinterpreted as threats or competition, and you are far more likely to have your fingers burned.

Whilst you may have identified the narcissist as a damaging individual, many people (particularly those under their control) will never be able to see the situation clearly. This can feel extremely unfair and unjust to those who can, particularly in family or romantic situations, if they are directly affected by narcissistic control, abuse or manipulation.

It is usually those people who "question" the status quo that the harmful narcissist finds most threatening, and subsequently suffer most acutely at their hands, as the narcissist feels compelled to bring them down to maintain their position. If the narcissist is a family member, particularly a parent, or a partner, this can be particularly damaging, with the victim often trained to unquestioningly agree or go along with the narcissist's opinions, to maintain their love and their favor. Those that follow receive their rewards, whilst those that question, are isolated, ridiculed and ousted, often labelled as a "black sheep," "troublesome" or "combative."

Avoid narcissistic injury

Sometimes, cutting the chord on a narcissistic relationship is not an option. You may feel you should at least try and continue a non-abusive relationship, in which case avoiding "narcissistic injury" is key to avoiding conflict.

In the minds of narcissistic people - both healthy and extreme - they are competent, have unique and special talents, and accomplished. In the case of healthy narcissists, any reasonable threat or challenge to these self-beliefs can be handled carefully, objectively, and in a proportionate way by the individual.

Threats to healthy narcissists don't include other successful or accomplished people - they may be positively competitive, but not derogatory. If a healthy narcissist takes a blow to their self-esteem, negative feelings may be processed without a melt-down or flying into a rage. Extreme narcissists, on the other hand, tend to exist in a world of hypervigilance. Any perceived threat or challenge is likely to be aggressively countered. Failing to do so could result in painful crashes to their self-esteem (narcissistic injury), as their opinion of themselves are overinflated, delicate and variable. This hypervigilance includes people they see as threatening, so it may be beneficial for you to lie low and purposely reduce the traits of your own that may make them feel competitive or badly about themselves.

Avoid exposing them

Exposing the narcissist and getting the "truth" out for all to see can be appealing and feel like the right thing to do. You may think this is the best solution for them, you and anyone else involved - that they will suddenly see clearly and take responsibility for changing their behavior. Forget about being right for a moment and bringing the truth to light.

Pointing out that the narcissist is not as wonderful as they think, can result in a huge backlash, that you then must be around, and may not be able to escape. They are not ever going to agree with you, as they are tied to their elevated identity. Rather than changing their minds, they will be more likely to simply despise you for your opinions.

Admire and listen to them

Being amenable is probably the most passive technique that you can take, but so long as you are not already on the narcissist's "naughty list" can be really effective at pulling you through difficult times, until you reach calmer waters or are able to end the relationship. Clinical psychologist Al Bernstein suggests that remaining quiet and allowing the narcissist to come up with reasons to congratulate themselves is easy, effortless and requires nothing more than listening and looking interested.

Admiring them, their achievements and qualities as much as they do can be a fast route into their "good books." So long as you avoid getting too close, this position in their good books can allow you to maintain a happier status quo with the narcissist still in your life.

Don't reject them

Rejecting a narcissist, whether in reality or in their perception, is likely to make them feel incredibly hurt or angry - as it causes a deep narcissistic injury. A jilted lover may feel a great deal of pain when the source of their affection no longer wants them. So, too, a narcissist feels deeply aggrieved when a source of narcissistic supply - or anyone else for that matter - decides that they are not "good enough."

Extreme narcissists – ever hypervigilant - may feel rejected for reasons that more average people would not. Being too busy or not having a good enough reason to deny their request for your company or collaboration can easily be taken to heart and result in an unexpectedly intense response. It's best to give them a legitimate reason that is beyond your control than to show that you're choosing to reject them.

Being too busy to meet or see them is best if your reason is irrefutable, like having to work late to meet a specific deadline, attend an important wedding, or are booked onto a vacation or trip elsewhere.

Avoid showing weakness

If you show a narcissist what it is that makes you vulnerable, or what it is that you really want, they may at some point use it against you when they want to manipulate you. Narcissists will frequently learn what it is that you want most from them, and set about denying it so that you are in a constant state of "need". If a narcissistic mother does this, she may control her children through their neediness for her love. The same goes for a romantic partner. They'll ration your supply of what you enjoy most from them to keep you controllable and pliable.

If they know your greatest concerns or fears they may leverage these to manipulate you. They may even use you as a distraction from their own inner turmoil when they are experiencing crashing self-esteem, by needling you on your points of weakness, to make themselves feel strong again.

For example, an NPD manager suffering a meltdown of anxiety after a disastrous sales pitch may proceed to milk his staff for reassurance on his performance, whilst then moving the conversation on to subjects that he knows are extremely personal and emotional for them - transferring his fears to them and feeling better himself.

By not conceding any weaknesses to a narcissist and always taking a diplomatic "I know I'll be happy either way" approach, their power will bring you down whilst raising themselves higher is lost. This may take on the appearance of a game of cat and mouse, until eventually the narcissist must concede that you are not "easily pinned" or risk exposing themselves and being seen as a pessimistic and negative person.

Give them an "out"

You can give them the opportunity to stop playing manipulative games by offering them an "out" such as: "You're being uncharacteristically pessimistic today. You're usually such an optimist! Is there anything wrong?" and in doing so call them to return to their "higher state of glory" without continuing their attack. Subconsciously, they may even be aware that you successfully navigated their manipulation and decide to give you a wider berth in future, or that they need to keep you on the side.

If the attack is particularly vicious or nasty, avoiding emotions but maintaining a cool, calm and empathic approach can work well to bring them back around. Whether you believe it or not, providing them with a defense that effectively excuses their behavior will be much appreciated - as it helps them to avoid a crushing sense of shame and subsequent denial loops, and simply feel that they are understood and forgiven. You may even be surprised to find that this approach results in a voluntary concession and what may seem like the beginnings or a more responsible approach, but this is not something that should be anticipated or expected.

Don't expect fairness

Extreme narcissists are likely to be far more concerned with getting what they want, than ensuring that everyone is treated fairly. Reward their behavior rather than their words so that they only get what they want, when you get what you want too.

Extending credit or accepting promises from an extreme narcissist is a dangerous leap of faith that may not be rewarded. Lack of follow through is just as likely to occur because the narcissist forgets their agreements - their attention being consumed with themselves and their own concerns rather than remembering their obligations.

They want to look good

Understanding what a narcissist wants means that so long as you avoid triggering narcissistic injury, they may be able to be worked with. You may even be able to maneuver them, if you start to think like them.

Extreme narcissists really want to look good. If you can align what they want with what you want, you may be able to achieve great successes together. Alternatively, you may simply be able to manage and placate them to make your life easier or until you are able to leave the relationship.

Understand their narcissistic supply

Narcissists need people to gain narcissistic supply. You might compare that a healthier person needs others for mutual love and support, but as we proceed higher up the extreme narcissism scale, the need becomes more one-directional and desperate in nature, to prevent painful relapses to a place of low self-esteem. So, what exactly do they want from you?

Highly narcissistic people often prioritize relationships and career choices based on how much praise or attention they can receive. Many narcissistic people hamper their own development (or never develop a range of interests in the first place), by making choices for praise and success over other forms of enjoyment. If they have chosen you as a part of their life, it may be that you provide a high level of narcissistic supply.

If you have not been chosen voluntarily, you may find that your relationship quality depends on how readily you give narcissistic supply, or whether you question or criticize them.

Taking responsibility for not damaging their wellbeing - whilst protecting your own - is as important for them as it is for anyone else. You would not feel great about filling the liquor cabinet in the home of an alcoholic, nor should you feel great about pedaling exorbitant approval and attention onto this already dependent individual. Moderate and considerate amounts to avoid attack or denigration is enough for you to get by.

An audience

Narcissists often want an audience. They may spend a great deal of time talking about themselves. This serves their need to feel special (since they are always the subject of the discussion). They also get to let other people know how much they have accomplished in life. And the result of this is that they get lots of praise from other people.

Status

Presuming they don't feel threatened by people of high status, they may want to associate with them in order to feel superior to others. If you think you classify as "high status", this may be what they are using you for. In this case - check your own score for narcissism. It is not unknown for narcissists to flock together and form superficial friendships and relationships to "show off" to others and highlight how special they both are, such as in a "trophy" partner / wealthy-partner relationship. Alternatively, they may want company from someone who is lower than they are to compare to themselves to, for a similar sense of superiority.

Some may choose a mix of friends - a bunch of successful equals to go out and "show off" with, and one or two best friends to feel superior to, to impress and revel in their attention.

Sex

It may be that the extreme narcissist does not engage in sexual relationships for the emotional value it has; but for sex, and sex alone. They may revel in their ability to seduce, in their sexual performance, or in a sense of higher status or dominance within the sexual dynamic.

Love

Narcissistic people like to feel that there is someone who loves them and wants to be with them. Depending on how they view themselves, this may result in higher levels of infidelity or cheating. If a narcissist defines themselves as "good" or "moral" then cheating itself (or engaging in any generally scorned upon activities) could result in crushing shame and self-loathing, making it less likely to happen. On the other hand, if the narcissist is reluctant to see their partner as an equal, the likelihood of cheating increases.

Avoid flooding them with supply

If you are concerned about providing a narcissist with supply, keeping them in line can be aligned more with what they don't want. Being all about appearances, narcissists feel more shame than guilt. They really don't want to look bad.

Asking them to consider their reputation may make them think far more carefully than asking them to consider other people's feelings. If they think their actions will be perceived badly by others, they are far less likely to act. This can be achieved by asking them what people would think about what they did or asking probing questions to trigger them into having an alternative idea themselves.

Chapter 10. Ways to Stop a Deceiver in Their Tracks

If you've read up to this point, then chances are you're probably thinking of a long list of people that have just got to be narcissists or deceivers in your life. However, as a caution: Not everyone is a narcissist just because you have a little tiff here and there. Also, keep in mind that you might be recollecting past events through the narcissistic glasses, and so everyone might seem to be that way.

With that said, if you've asked yourself the questions listed in this book, and have observed for yourself that you really are dealing with a deceiver, how do you deal with them? Let's get into that.

Putting an End to Gaslighting

Pay attention to the pattern. One of the major reasons gaslighting is so effective is that, for the most part, the target is completely ignorant of what's happening. The minute you move from ignorance to complete awareness, you will have successfully taken back some of your power. You will find it easier to shrug off the narcissist when they start playing games again.

Keep in mind that the deceiver might never change, no matter what you do. Sometimes, the only way there can be any change is with the help of a professional. Gaslighting is all that the manipulator knows how to do, so you cannot expect them to give that up in favor of logic or reason. There is no other better coping mechanism that they know. This is not to say that they should not be held accountable for their actions. I'm just making sure you now not to hold on to the hope that they will change. They could, but don't hope for it. Accept that they're wired the way they are, and only professional therapy can help them become better people.

Remember that gaslighting behavior is not necessarily about you. It all really comes down to the fact that the deceiver needs to feel like they're in charge. They need that rush of power. At their core, the deceiver is riddled with insecurity. The only way they know how to get rid of that feeling is to make others feel less than they are, or at least give themselves the illusion that they are better than everyone else. Keep this in mind, and you will not bother internalizing anything they say or do anymore. You will be in a better position to manage the relationship you have with them or to end it altogether.

Create a support system that you can rely on. Dealing with a deceiver on your own is no walk in the park. It helps to have other people that you can talk to, who will validate your perception of reality as well as your sense of self-worth. If you've noticed that ever since you got involved with the narcissist, you've somehow been cut off from the people that matter to you, then now is the time to reach out to them. Do not buy into the narcissist's lies about how no one else can love you the waythey do. That is simply not true! Commit to spending time with your friends and family. Make appointments, if you must. Treat these appointments with as much commitment as you would a business meeting. The less isolated you are, the less of a hold the deceiver can have on you.

Spend a long time thinking about whether you want to keep investing in the relationship. This is crucial, especially since having to deal with the deceiver's shenanigans eats away at your peace of mind, self-worth - and even your health. Is the deceiver your manager, or your boss? Then take proactive steps to find another job, making it a non-negotiable agreement with yourself that you're moving to a different, better job. If the deceiver is your lover and you'd like the relationship to continue, then keep in mind that you'll both be needing some therapy, and you will have to make that a non-negotiable aspect of your relationship if you decide to stay.

Start to build your self-esteem back up. Having been with a deceiver for too long, it's easy to forget just how awesome you are! You need to take some time to remind yourself of everything about you that is amazing, no matter what the deceiver has said to make you think otherwise. You might need to begin journaling so that at times when you are low or starting to buy into the insidious lies they have packed your head with, you can reopen that, and remind yourself of your awesomeness. Don't just write about the great things about you. Write about times when you felt the most alive, the most joyful. As you do this, you will naturally find yourself craving those times again, and taking action to liberate yourself and your mind.

Be open to getting professional help. It's difficult being the victim of gaslighting. Your self-esteem, sense of self, and sanity will have taken a beating. You might find that you're slow to make decisions, constantly unsure of yourself, and always wondering if you're good enough. You might even be suffering from depression or anxiety. If you find that you're overwhelmed by feelings of helplessness, uncertainty, hopelessness, and apathy, then chances are you need to seek the help of a professional psychotherapist right away, so that you can rebuild yourself after the devastating damage caused to you by the deceiver

Change Is Possible

There it is. The answer you've been hoping for, waiting for with bated breath: it's possible for people to change, no matter what personality disorder they have been diagnosed with. Think of these diagnoses as a shorthand way of describing certain people. You can never use one word to totally encapsulate a person's life. When words like extrovert, introvert, or narcissist get bandied about, they seem to imply a permanence to the individual's personality. That's not always the case.

It helps to consider that these disorders are not necessarily descriptions of who people are in summary. It would be more accurate to think of these labels as the perfect descriptions for behavioral and/or inter-relational patterns, and nothing more. The same applies to narcissistic personalities.

Born of Vulnerability

A lot of researchers are of the opinion that Narcissistic Personality Disorder is a result of growing up in conditions where it's not safe to be vulnerable. The narcissist as a child had to accept that it was a sign of imperfection to be vulnerable, and that showing any vulnerability meant that they had no worth at all. This theory is the reason there's often a connection made between insecure attachment styles and narcissism, meaning the narcissist is driven to control all their relationships because they are afraid to be in a position where they need to depend on someone else.

The narcissist is adept at keeping people from knowing who they really are. They will refuse to acknowledge their vulnerabilities or opt to suppress them or project them onto others so that they can keep crafting the person they want to be in relation to others. For the narcissist to change, they must be willing to be vulnerable. This means leaving themselves wide open to emotions that they have suppressed and denied over the years. The trouble with narcissists is not that they are unable to change, it's that they are *unwilling to* because it would mean that the identity of the person they have struggled to craft will be blown to bits. In a narcissist's mind, all the relationships which they have failed at simply offer more reason why they should remain the way they are.

Understand that the narcissist defines themselves by how others perceive them. A narcissist can't be a narcissist if they don't have anyone to put on a show for. They need to be the center of attention, and so they love to have the spotlight of attention from those who bother to stick around them. Over time, of course, their performance starts to get old. The narcissist knows this and is constantly running scared that others will realize there's really nothing to them. This is one of the reasons the narcissist refuses to change, as they are more certain than ever that the fix is not to come clean and be vulnerable but to put on a more flamboyant show and pile on some more makeup to conceal all their flaws.

When the Narcissist Finds True, Secure Love

When the narcissist happens to find someone who cares about them and is not just sticking around for the flash, they're still deathly afraid that this person will think they're not worth it. The fear they feel is a subconscious one that they are not aware of, but it is very real. This is what fuels the narcissist to do things like shift blame and guilt onto their partner or act all grandiose.

When their antics are exposed to the light of day, and everyone sees them for what they are, they get angry because they've slipped up and alienated everyone who mattered to them. Rather than change their ways, this causes them to double down on who they are. They become even more narcissistic than ever before, ironically leading to the abandonment and rejection that they're so afraid of.

Breaking the Cycle

To help the narcissist, there's nothing else to do but break that vicious cycle. As gently as you can, you need to throw a wrench in the works whenever they try to control you, create distance between you, blame you, or defend themselves. This means letting them know in no uncertain terms that you're willing to have them in your life, but not on those terms. What terms, then? You should show them that they can join you in the sort of intimacy where they can be loved for who they really are, flaws and all. They only need to be willing to let that happen.

The point to take away from all of this is that narcissism is simply one way of relating to others, and you can always change the way you relate with people. It's not going to be easy for narcissists to let themselves get so vulnerable as to allow intimacy, but it is possible.

The Narcissist to who wants to Change

If you happen to know someone who's a narcissist but has expressed the willingness to do better, then you can let them read the book. Here is a list of things the narcissist will need to do to become a better person. This is addressed to the narcissist, not the victim.

Learn to recognize and respect boundaries. When you do, you'll find that you stop losing relationships, and improve them. You must understand where you end, and another begins. You need to understand that other people have their own beliefs, thoughts, and emotions, and they can be completely different from yours while remaining valid. To help you understand boundaries better:

- Listen twice as much as you speak.

- Use other people's names when you write to them, and when you speak to them, too.

- Get curious about the people around you. Ask questions to learn what matters to them and what's new in their lives. Don't be inappropriate in your asking.

- Be mindful of encroaching into other people's personal space and time. Always ask permission first before you do.

- Rather than issue orders, ask open questions. Don't ask leading questions. Don't assume you know better than others.

- When others make a choice that is different from yours, respect it. You won't always get what you want, and that's okay.

Be genuine, always, in all ways. You will find it more refreshing than lying, pretending, and manipulating others. How can you be more genuine?

- Keep your word. If you know you won't keep a promise, don't make it.

- Did you make a promise you can't follow through on? Then own it.

- Don't say or do things that will make others feel like they've been cheated.

Observe yourself often so you can grow in mindfulness. The more you observe, the better you can see how you cause problems in your relationships and push people away. Assume that there's the usual you, and then there's your higher self who observes you from a higher point of view. Here's how to be more mindful:

- Ask your higher or observer self whether whatever you're about to say or do will have good or bad consequences.

- Ask your observer self if your actions and words are all about you showing off, or about you building a great relationship with others.

- Feel like you just did or said something off? Ask your observer self how it would feel if someone said or did that to you. Then apologize and make amends quickly.

Be willing to seek professional help. This will help you along your journey to becoming a more rounded individual, faster. You don't have to struggle with this on your own. You need the guidance of a psychotherapist. You need to be willing to be honest if you're going to make permanent, lasting change. It's going to be so worth it in the end because you will finally discover your authentic self, and your relationships will be better for it.

Do forgive yourself. This is the only way to get the healing you need. It's also the only way that you can be more comfortable with being vulnerable. An added plus is you'll finally be able to flex those empathy muscles. It might be hard to forgive yourself, and you may find yourself crippled with remorse sometimes. Just be kind to yourself in moments like this. You only did the best you knew to do so that you could cope. It's not your fault that you weren't allowed to be your true self when you were growing up. Focus on the fact that now, you can do better. Now, you can rediscover yourself.

Be okay with being human. You won't be perfect. You never were. You have flaws, but that's okay! Learn to be comfortable in your own skin. This is the way to allow rich, beneficial, loving relationships in your life; this is how you grow. You simply need to be fine with who you are. Be okay with being true to yourself, even if it means being vulnerable.

It's going to take you some time. Be patient. You will find yourself. You will also learn that the thing you feared the most is not real. The people who love you don't up and leave just because of imperfection or five. After all, we're all flawed in our own way.

The Trouble with Emotional Abuse

The trouble with emotional abuse is that because it leaves no scars, you can see, it often gets dismissed, or is almost impossible to spot when it happens. Make no mistake: the damage from emotional abuse is very real, and it can last a long, long time.

When you're psychologically abused, the other person is saying and doing things to make you think whatever they want. Generally, the goal is to make you confused, disillusioned, and totally dependent on them for your sense of self-worth and identity. It is an incredibly hurtful, despicable thing to do to another person, and can lead to very real mental health issues like depression, Post-Traumatic Stress Disorder, and anxiety.

Unmasking Emotional Abuse

There are a lot of myths about emotional abuse, which do a very good job of camouflaging it so that it's hard to detect. Let's rip the mask off, so you can have an easier time figuring out whether you or someone you care about is being abused.

Myth #1: Emotional abuse is always accompanied by physical abuse.
It isn't. There can be emotional abuse with no physical abuse; this often flies under the radar.

Myth #2: Emotional abuse is nowhere near as damaging as physical abuse. This is just pure falsehood. If it hurts, then it hurts. It is not a productive argument to say that one form of abuse hurts more than another. Abuse is not okay. If you're being abused, then you deserve better, and you need all the help you can get.

Myth #3: Emotional abuse only affects women. Abuse can happen to both women and men. There is no exception. Also, it happens in other contexts besides relationships, such as at work, and with friends as well.

What to Do If You're Being Abused

If you're emotionally abused, then you're constantly criticized for everything you say and do. You're blamed all the time, even for things that could never be your fault. You're made to feel ashamed. Your deceiver constantly threatens to hurt you physically or to do something they know you don't want them to. You feel like you have zero control over your life, as the abuser takes all your power away, sometimes even going as far as controlling your finances so that you have no choice but to stay with them and do whatever they want.

If you recognize yourself in the paragraph above, then you need to do something. You need to reach out and ask for help. There is no shame in that. As a matter of fact, asking for help is one of the bravest things you can possibly do, especially when you're in a situation where you have been completely worn down and out by the abuser.

Talk to anyone you can about what you're going through. Confide in them, and not only will you have someone on your side, but you will also be able to occupy your time by hanging out with others besides your abuser. Work on getting more and more people you can talk to who will back you up.

Have a safety plan in place. While there's not necessarily physical abuse going on along with the emotional abuse, it's still important to be safe. This means you need to think up plans for how you can escape from the relationship whenever you are finally ready to up and leave the abuser.

Don't Make Excuses for the Abuse

A lot of the time, people will fall back on mental disorders in order to justify when they do what they do. They don't talk about it like they want to make genuine change. It's just a copout for them to keep treating you the way that they always have.

It's not uncommon for the person abusing you to try to make light of the situation or try to blame you for a reason they're acting the way they do. It can seem like your significant other doesn't know when they do what they do or are completely incapable of realizing the implications of their actions. However, this is just more smoke and mirrors on their part. They know what they're doing. The whole point behind being seemingly unaware is to make you feel even less sure of yourself. Next thing you know, you start wondering if you're not overly dramatic or delusional! I want you to know that your abusive partner is very aware of how they're hurting you, and they always are in control of how they act disorder or no. Want proof?

They will decide when to abuse you, and how far they will push it. A perfect example is when they threaten to hit you but don't. Or when they abuse you in ways that you can never really tell others, because there's no proof, and it can seem like you're making something out of nothing.

They only ever abuse you, not others. If they truly had no control over their actions, wouldn't they abuse everyone in their lives? But they don't, do they? That's because they can control themselves. If it were that they suffered from a disorder, then everyone in their life would get the same treatment, and not just you.

They escalate their terrible behavior. When it's a matter of having a disorder, there can be changes in the person's state of mind. Even then, though, there is a consistency in the way that they behave. However, you may have noticed your abuser will sometimes choose not to abuse you for a while. Other times, they will steadily ramp up the abuse as your relationship goes on. This is more proof that they really can decide to be different or better.

You need to keep in mind that regardless of whether the deceiver has an actual mental health problem, you are not the one to be held accountable for how they treat you! It's possible to be diagnosed with a disorder and still choose not to act out in controlling, manipulative ways. They will simply need to acknowledge their issues and be open and willing to seek the help that they need. Please, always remember that you're not the reason they act the way they do, and therefore you're not the cure they need. They must own their actions, and they alone can take the first step they need, to change themselves.

Chapter 11. A Match Made in Hell: Narcissists And Empaths

There is one specific union which is never going to end well. We are of course talking about the match between a narcissist and an empath. The reason is that both are at totally opposite ends of the empathy spectrum, and as a result, they clash constantly.

This chapter is going to explore why narcissists and empaths are a terrible match, but we're also going to discuss the fact that this is a match which happens more often than you would think.

First things first, we need to explore what an empath is, to really understand why this union is one to avoid at all costs.

What is an Empath?

There is a difference between someone who is an empath and someone who possesses empathy. A person who has empathy can understand the feelings of others and put themselves in their shoes. This is most people, but everyone varies with the degree of empathy they have. Someone can be a highly sensitive person, e.g. have a high amount of empath, but that still doesn't make them an empath.

An empath is someone who is extremely sensitive to the emotions of others, to the point where they take them on as their own. For example, an empath may be standing next to someone in the line for the bus, and that person may be feeling angry about something that has happened that morning. As a result, the empath will begin to feel angry, but they have no reason to feel angry themselves. They're picking up on the vibrations and emotions of the other person and exhibiting that emotion as their own.

Empaths are not rare, and many people have this tendency in their lives. Whilst it is considered a gift, the person who has it may not consider it so! Life can become very overwhelming for people who are so sensitive to emotions around them, and many empaths find large groups to be very draining. As a result, they will either avoid large gatherings or will leave quite early.

An empath also has to find ways to manage their "gift" in order to stop it taking over their lives.

In addition to being sensitive to emotions, empaths are also drawn to people who are in need. Empaths are very pure and positive people, and they like to help others who may be going through a hard time or maybe suffering in some way but not vocalizing it. The problem occurs when an empath cannot draw a line between their own emotions and the emotions of another person, and they find it extremely difficult to walk away from those in their life, simply because they can feel their pain and their general emotions.

The main traits of an empath are:

- Usually introverted but can be extroverted too,
- Like their own space and time alone,
- Can become overwhelmed in large groups,
- Highly sensitive,
- Very intuitive,
- Can easily become overwhelmed when in a relationship and needs to learn how to step back a little and take their own space whenever needed,
- Often give too much of themselves, as they normally have big hearts,
- Their senses are highly attuned,
- They often need to be around nature to feel calm.

Aside from absorbing the emotions of others like a sponge, one of the biggest risks of having this empathic gift is the fact that empaths are a huge target for narcissists and other "energy vampires". An energy vampire is someone who is very negative or someone who is very manipulative and finds it easy to literally suck the life out of an empath, who is willing to give to the point of exhaustion. To protect themselves against such people, empaths need to have plenty of time and space to themselves.

Why Are Narcissists And Empaths Drawn to Each Other?

Now we know what an empath is, why are empaths and narcissists a common coupling?

There is an attraction on both sides here. Firstly, the empaths recognize the struggle of the narcissist, e.g. their lack of confidence and their underlying struggles. The empath can feel this but they also have a nurturing side which makes them want to make things better. Of course, we know that nobody can make a narcissist better, but the empath wants to try.

In addition, narcissists are, as we know, extremely charming and can trick people into thinking they're a wonderful person, when underneath they may have other intentions. Because an empath always wants to see the best in people, they have a tendency for falling for the charm. You would think that their intuition would allow them to see past this smokescreen, but the narcissist is an expert at deception and often manages to slip beneath the radar.

The reason a narcissist is attracted to an empath is because of their opposite nature. Remember, narcissists, don't have empathy like a non-narcissistic person. An empath is totally the opposite and has empathy by the bucket-load. This intrigues the narcissist, but they can also see that this may be a person who can easily be manipulated. As a result, the narcissist makes a bee-line for the empath, showing their full charm armory.

Whilst every relationship is different, the chances are that a union between a narcissist and an empath will follow a very common path. The narcissist will charm the empath completely, and the empath will fall completely underneath their spell. The narcissist will then begin their gaslighting techniques as the empath begins to show their confidence and tries to have their own life outside of the relationship.

The empath struggles to understand why the narcissist is causing them distress because they look for the best in everyone. As a result, the narcissist uses tactics to make the empath question their own thoughts and feelings, which is confusing because they're already overwhelmed with emotions, due to their empathic nature.

Empaths feel everything very deeply, so when the narcissist hurts the empath, they will feel it ten times amplified. This causes a rollercoaster relationship to begin, with ups and downs, crazy highs and crashing lows. The highs and lows are addictive, and the endless gaslighting and charm offensive make them stay.

A relationship between a narcissist and empath is very similar to a relationship between a narcissist and a regular person, however, the difference is the depth of feelings that an empath experiences. As a result, they will have highs and lows which exhaust them, and when this occurs in conjunction with all the other emotions they're picking up on a day to day basis, the effect can be extremely damaging.

Is There a Future For This Relationship?

Put simply, no. There is less chance of this relationship surviving compared to any other narcissistic-affected relationship. The emotional highs and lows, along with the dependency which the empath will develop toward the narcissist will make the relationship impossible to survive.

The empath will have a very hard time leaving the narcissist, and it will probably take several attempts to actually go through with it. Despite that, it is hoped that the empath eventually finds the strength to walk away.

This type of relationship has no future. The narcissist will drain every last drop of positive out of the empath and leave them completely overwhelmed, emotionally confused, and they will question their sanity to the point of exhaustion.

Of course, the empath will desperately want to "fix" the narcissist and they will try time and time again to do it. In the end, however, they will realize that it's just not possible and they will give up and move on - at least, that is the hope.

How an Empath Can be Severely Emotionally Damaged by a Narcissist

A narcissist will use the empath's emotional sensitivity against them. This is a weak point in the eyes of the narcissist, and something they don't really understand themselves. Being able to feel everything so deeply is so intoxicating to the narcissist, so exotic and different, that they want to explore it and find out more about it. They then realize that this is an "in", something they can use alongside their gaslighting tactics, and it works very successfully.

An empath is generally a very pure and good person. They try to help and they try to see the good in others, but their emotional sensitivity is their undoing in this situation. They also try time and time again to right the situation, to make the narcissist see the error of their ways, to show them that they understand and want to help, but remember, the narcissist sees no error in their ways. In the eyes of the narcissist, they're not the one to blame, the empath is. By blaming the empath, they are damaging their self-esteem and their self-worth to a very severe degree.

The constant bombardment of gaslighting, making the empath feel like they're literally going crazy, will work completely against the overwhelming feeling of experiencing emotions outside of their own head. As a result, the empath may suffer an emotional breakdown, due to complete exhaustion.

An empath will struggle severely with a relationship touched by narcissism because it is something they simply cannot understand themselves. Both sides are totally at odds - the narcissist doesn't understand the emotional sensitivity of the empath and the empathy they show with almost everything they do. The empath doesn't understand the narcissist's total lack of empathy and how they can be so cold and unforgiving, yet so charming and giving when they want to turn on the act. The empath may know that something isn't right, they may want to walk away, but their need to see the good in everyone keeps them where they shouldn't be.

Put simply, an empath could suffer mental health damage by staying in a relationship with a narcissist, and that will take professional help to right and overcome. They will struggle with building lasting, trusting relationships in the future, and they may also turn against their emotional sensitivity and empathy, and see it as a hindrance, rather than a positive trait or a gift.

A narcissist has the power to destroy an empath.

Points to Take From This Chapter

In this chapter, we have explored the damaging relationship between a narcissist and an empath. You might not have known much about empaths before this chapter, but now the hope is that you understand much more.

Perhaps you're an empath, or you're very emotionally sensitive yourself. In that case, you need to be very wary of anyone in your life who might be exploring your sensitivity. A narcissist will see an empath as easy pickings, a real target, and someone who is easy to manipulate. To be able to turn the tables, you need to identify the signs, and you also need to develop the strength to walk away.

The main points to take from this chapter are:

• An empath is someone who is very emotionally sensitive and can take on the emotions of others as their own;

• Empaths are usually introverted, quiet, kind people, who try to see the best in everyone;

- Empaths can also become overwhelmed by emotions very easily, and they feel everything very deeply;

- Narcissists are attracted to empaths because they are curious about their empathy, but also because they may see them as an easy target;

- Empaths are attracted to narcissists because they want to help, but also because they're a target for the charm offensive which often comes at the start of a relationship;

- A relationship with a narcissist may be enough to cause an empath to have an emotional breakdown or burn out reaction if the manipulation is severe enough;

- The empath will feel the hurt and pain of the treatment by a narcissist very deeply, but will still want to do their best to help their partner;

- Empaths are likely to need a lot of help and support when walking away from a narcissistic partner and may heed professional help in order to allow them to develop loving and trusting relationships in the future.

Chapter 12 – How to stop being manipulated by a deceiver

Gaslighting has become a hot topic today because it is a harmful manipulation tool either an emotional, psychological manipulation thing that is happening to many people than we even realize. So before now, we have really talked about what gas-lighting is and how do you know that you have been a victim of gaslighting and the tactics that deceivers use.

As stated before, gaslighting is a subtle way of somebody avoiding responsibility after that person has done something bad. In extreme cases, it is a way to emotionally abused or gain power over somebody in harmful ways. If you haven't read the chapter that talks about the signs of gaslighting or how to know if you are being gaslighted, then go and do that now because if you haven't done that, then you won't really understand what this chapter is saying. It won't make sense if you don't recognize what gaslighting is and if you don't realize that it is happening to you. So we are going to talk about some ways to deal with gaslighting.

Clarify yourself

And the first thing is to clarify to yourself how you know you're being gaslighted and then write it down. Write down the specific things that is done or said to you that make you know that you are being gaslighted. Write down specific examples as they come up and write down the things that this person is making you feel crazy, question yourself on, make you feel like you are losing it and making you question your own sanity. Those people use certain tasks to Gaslight you. It is leaking and it's up to and if you're not aware of what the person is doing, you might not even realize that it is happening to you.

Do some ground exercise

The next one it's for you to start doing some grounding exercises and just take time to be quiet and be still with yourself so that you can start connecting with yourself again. You might take some time to do some deep breathing. Whatever those grounding and meditating exercise is do it to start connecting with yourself again, because gaslighting makes you doubt and question yourself. It makes you. Believing yourself.

It makes you feel like you can trust yourself again. So you need to start taking time to connect with yourself, again, you need to take the time to start tuning into your inner wisdom and tune to your ability to believe and trust yourself. Because that has been taken away from you, if you haven't gaslighted for a long time at some point in your life, you really need to reconnect with yourself so that you can start to realize that you are being manipulated. You need to be able to trust yourself and see that this person is meant to mess with you and to throw you off. So, you need to get things backgrounded by taking the time to connect with yourself in your thoughts, your beliefs, your perceptions and really ground yourself in that stuff.

Decide whether you want to continue the relationship

The next one is if it is someone that is currently in your life that is any plating you this week, and if it is becoming a big issue, then you might need to decide whether you want to continue the relationship. So you really need to decide if you need to distance yourself from this person or discontinue the relationship altogether. This is a very serious thing when you are being made to feel small weak or made to feel insignificant, stupid, crazy, insane, then you really need to take it seriously and decide if it is worth it to continue in that relationship. Even though there are certain times that these people will be caring, loving, and wonderful and allow you to have a great moment with them. But other times, they try to make you feel small, stupid or crazy, so you really need to listen to yourself and really decide if it is worth it. Decide if that person is worthy of staying in your life since that is how they are treating you and making you feel low and taking away from you your ability to feel confident in yourself.

Reach out to a trusted loved one or friend

The next thing to do is to reach out to somebody like a friend or a trusted loved one and tell that person because; chances are if you have been a victim of gaslighting for a long period. And it has really ever affected your sense of self-worth and ability to trust yourself; then you need to do some healing that is not just going to go away. You really need to dig into it because things like that will start to impact your core believes. It will start to manipulate your self-worth, so you need that intervention to be able to heal from it and be able to move forward from the wounds, the pains, the hurt, and the damage that this might have caused you. So this is something that you really need to take seriously.

Take a Stand

The last one is to take a stand and not let yourself continue to be a victim. Once you recognize that the gaslighting is happening, then you want to be able to see what the person is doing. You need to stand up to them and say something like I see what you doing and I'm not going to fall for it. No matter how hard they try to convince you, and no matter which Tactics they're using, try to stand up to them and say that that's not what happened, you are lying, you are making this stuff up. Try to take a stand and take your power back instead of being a victim or allowing yourself to get manipulated or even abused in this harmful way.

If you're doing some of these things and implementing some of these strategies, then it will help you to be able to regain your personal sense of clarity, and then you will start to trust yourself again. You will be able to connect with yourself and even to believe in yourself, and you will be able to trust your senses, your memories, your perceptions, and your version and your interpretation of reality, and you will be able to put a stop to people that are playing the mind games with you.

Having healthy boundaries is very good in any area of your life especially when it comes to Gaslight. You need to put in those boundaries, say no way, this is not going to happen to me, and no way am I going to fall for this. I'm not going to let you treat me this way. Having healthy boundaries is Crucial.

Dealing with the Narcissist

Now that you've realized that there is a narcissist in your life, what should you do?

Take a step back and analyze the situation.

Determine how bad the situation is. Try to understand the narcissist's background and his degree of his narcissism. Note or recall what drives him to narcissistic rage. Recall how he tries to punish you. Be aware of the tactics that he uses. Do all these objectively. Being carried away by emotions, shouting or crying will only feed the narcissist. The narcissist has already painstakingly set up a strong image or reputation and you might not come across as credible when you tell others, so you have to do your homework.

Accept that the narcissist will not change.

Hoping that you will be able to knock some sense into the narcissist or that you could explain and things to enlighten him will not work. As far as the narcissist is concerned, he has done no wrong.

Seek help.

Find people – friends, counselors, religious leaders, or parents- any one you can confide in and who can give advice and emotional support. They can also give feedback from a neutral viewpoint.

Set boundaries.

Write down which boundaries the narcissist cannot trespass and a consequence if they do. Writing things down before talking to the narcissist will help you speak without sounding emotional.

Be realistic.

Know the narcissist's limitations and work within those limits. It will only be emotionally draining and a waste of time to expect more from the narcissist than he is capable. Do not expect him to learn to care because he can't.

Remember that your value as a person does not depend on the narcissist.

Don't punish yourself for getting into a relationship with him. Instead, focus on rebuilding your self-esteem, meeting your own needs and pursuing your interests.

Speak to them in a way that will make them aware of how they will benefit.

Instead of voicing you needs, pleading, crying or yelling; learn to rephrase your statements by emphasizing what the narcissist will gain from it. You have learn to appeal to their selfishness. This is a good way to survive in situations when you cannot leave.

Bring up your ideas to the narcissistic boss when there are witnesses. By having others around to hear your idea, he will find it difficult to claim credit for it.

Find proof of or document any kind of abuse.

Make use of technology- CCTV or video recordings, for example- to document instances of abuse. Find witnesses to back you up.

Do not fall for the narcissist's tactics again.

Refresh yourself on his tactics and be on your guard against falling for them again. The narcissist may try to use pity, projection or hoovering. This time, be wiser. It may take practice, as you may have become used to being the "Echo" or codependent. Being aware will help you to resist.

Leave.

The best way to deal with the narcissist is not to. For the sake of you emotional and physical well-being, not to mention your sanity, it would be best to leave. If you do leave, expect various tactics from the narcissist to either make your life miserable or to get you (actually his supply) back. You will also undergo a period of distress, akin to mourning when you leave. Seek help and support to get through this stage. Do not be hard on yourself for having allowed yourself to be deceived by the narcissist. Your experience will make you stronger, wiser and, in time, ready for a healthy relationship. In the meantime, focus on your own interests and rebuilding your self-esteem.

Chapter 13- Narcissistic Personality Disorder

A narcissistic personality disorder is a disease that affects approximately 1% of the population with a higher incidence of males than females. It is characterized by excessive arrogance, lack of empathy and a great need for admiration. The main marker of a narcissistic personality is grandiosity. They are interested in power, prestige, and vanity and believe that they deserve special treatment.

Narcissistic personality disorder should not be confused with a person with high self-esteem. A person with high self-esteem can be humble, while a narcissist cannot. They are selfish, overconfident, and ignore the feelings and needs of others. Also, the disorder has a negative impact on a person's life. In general, one may be dissatisfied with one's life and be disappointed when others do not admire it and are not given the special attitude or care it needs. All vital areas are affected (work, personal, social ...), but one is not able to realize that their behavior negatively affects their relationships. People do not feel comfortable with a narcissistic person and they will feel dissatisfied with their work, their social life, etc.

Symptoms and characteristics of narcissistic personality disorder

Some Of the Symptoms and Characteristics of a Narcissistic Personality These are:

- Concern for fantasies, successes ...

- Faith, which is of great importance, only feels understood and connected to people who believe they have high status.

- They need and require continuous admiration.

- Exaggeration of your achievements and abilities.

- Feel for rights or privileges.

- To envy others and have too much conviction that others envy.

- Think and talk most of the time in yourself.

- Suggest unrealistic goals.

- The expectations of others to provide special services.

- I believe that no one can question their motives and demands.

- Take advantage of others to get what they want without the hassle.

- Arrogance, arrogance.

- Easily rejected and injured.

- Strong desire.

- Responding to criticism with shame, indignation, and humiliation.

Narcissistic personality disorder: causes

There is no definite cause for narcissistic personality disorder, but researchers agree that there are environmental and genetic factors that play a role in the development of the disease.

Some of the genetic factors show that people with a narcissistic personality have less gray matter in the left insula, the part of the brain associated with empathy, emotional regulation, compassion, and cognitive functioning.

The healthy development of man shapes many of the narcissistic personality traits. Researchers believe that the onset of the disorder can occur when there is a conflict in interpersonal development. Some examples of contextual factors that may change the developmental stages of "normal" include:

- Learn manipulative behavior from parents or friends.

- To be overly praised for appropriate behavior and overly criticized for inappropriate behavior.

- You suffer from childhood abuse.

- Incompatible parental care.

- Being very pampered by parents, friends, family ...

- To be too delightful without realistic feedback.

- Receive many compliments from parents or others about their appearance or abilities.

Narcissistic personality disorder: treatment

Psychotherapy

Psychotherapy is one of the keys to approaching the treatment of narcissistic personality. It is usually used to help a person connect with other people more adaptively and gain a better understanding of their own and others' emotions.

If a person has a narcissistic personality, you may not have heard of the diagnosis. Studies show that they usually do not receive treatment, and if they receive it, progress is slow because it is based on personality traits that have formed over the years. Therefore, it takes years of psychotherapy to make changes. The changes aim to take responsibility for their actions and to learn ways to connect more appropriately. This includes:

- You are accepting and maintaining relationships with classmates and family.
- They tolerate criticism and failure.
- Understand and regulate feelings.
- Minimize the desire to achieve unrealistic goals.

Initially, group therapy was thought to be inappropriate because group therapy requires empathy, patience, and the ability to relate to and "connect" with others, something in which a person with narcissistic personality disorder presents with deficits. However, studies show that long-term group therapy can benefit them by providing a safe context where they can talk about their boundaries, receive and give feedback, and raise awareness of themselves and their problems.

Of cognitive-behavioral therapy, in particular, the scheme-focused treatment produces excellent results. It focuses on restoring narcissistic schemas and strategies to deal with them while confronting narcissistic cognitive styles (perfectionism ...).

treatment

There is no specific treatment for this disease, but sometimes these people may experience depression or anxiety, and psychotropic medications can be helpful. People with a narcissistic personality can abuse drugs or alcohol, so treating addictive problems can be something useful in this disorder.

Criteria for Narcissistic Personality Disorder

1. The exaggerated notion of personal importance not based on reality.

An inflated view of oneself is one of the main ways narcissists give themselves permission to dominate and control others. Narcissists believe that their priorities, interests, opinions, and beliefs have more value and are more important than anyone else's. Not all narcissists show the world their grandeur; some appear to be very humble or even shy to the outside world, but when they are in intimacy, this will dominate their coexistence.

2. The concern with fantasies of success, wealth, power, beauty, and love above normal.

Narcissists often have a fantasy-filled life and are rarely satisfied with the ordinary, however satisfying or beautiful it may be. This preoccupation with fantasy prevents the narcissistic personality from leading a real and stable life. They feed desires for wealth, fame, power, or status obsessively.

3. The belief that you are a special and unique individual, and can only be committed to or understood by special people.

This idea is an integral part of a survival mechanism that helps them cope with the world. They often define themselves by what they consider their special qualities and inform us of those qualities as soon as we know them.

4. The intense need for admiration.

Love me, watch me, pay attention to me. Narcissists tend to magnify and be their reference.

5. Feeling of worthiness.

Normal rules, regulations, and patterns of behavior infuriate narcissists, who think they are so unique that they do not have to obey reasonable expectations or respect appropriate limits. They may be equally plagued by hard work, illness, or injury. On the other hand, the rules that are imposed by them on others must always be respected.

6. The tendency to exploit others without feeling guilt or remorse.

Depending on the other characteristics of his personality, the narcissist may induce us to do all his work for him or, for example, take our money, allow us to pay his bills, receive gifts without ever giving, charge more for services and pay less, leave waiting for hours around the corner in the rain, without considering that this behavior is disrespectful. Your sense of worthiness makes these behaviors normal, preventing them from feeling guilty or remorseful.

7. Lack of significant empathy.

The narcissist has very little ability to put himself in someone else's shoes. Your pain, your problems, and your point of view dominate the universe. Perhaps nothing more reflects the narcissist's behavior than the inability to understand and identify with the experience of others. This is particularly true when the person who needs understanding is someone the narcissist is exploring, that is, his current target (loving, working, family, or friend).

8. The tendency to be envious or to imagine oneself the envy of others.

The narcissist has difficulty adjusting to a world in which other people seem to have "more" or "better" things. Narcissists often fail to recognize that they are envious and turn sentiment into contempt.

9. Arrogance.

Narcissists often have a snobby attitude toward people they think are not up to their "high" standard of intelligence, competence, accomplishment, values, morals, or lifestyle. Believing that the other is inferior helps them reinforce and inflate their conviction of superiority. Criticizing and diminishing others make them feel good about themselves. They are often homophobic, racist, prejudiced of all kinds simply because they think they are superior to a specific group.

Characteristics of narcissistic personality disorder

1. The excessive vision of the self, rather than a solid self-confidence, reflects an excessive concern for supposed excellence.

2. Active and competitive when looking for status, since their personal value is measured according to the status they have

3. If others do not recognize that status, they think they deserve, and they feel intolerable mistreated, get angry, become defensive, or depressed. If they are not known as superiors, their belief of inferiority and lack of importance is activated.

4. He is, therefore, hypersensitive and experiences very intense feelings in response to the criticisms of others.

5. They need, at all costs, the recognition of people whom they consider essential.

6. They do not tolerate discomfort or negative affection. They reject the vital circumstances that require a certain sacrifice and tolerance towards others such as marriage, and he thinks that he does not have to make concessions and yield to the other.

7. If limits are placed or criticized they become very unpleasant and defensive.

8. They show a very demanding and insensitive appearance, show little interest in emotionally supporting the other. They are very difficult to influence and are characterized by being great exploiters.

9. When others react to their exploitation and get angry with him, the narcissist thinks that what happens to him is that they are jealous of him.

10. Carefree of the feelings of others, very self-centered. When they have a conversation with others, they can give the feeling of unique personal interest. Although they can be warm in a first interaction, they immediately show arrogance, hurtful comments towards each other or insensitive actions.

11. They often envy the successes of others and discredit the people they see as competitors. Spend a lot of time comparing yourself to others

12. The worth of others lies in the ability of others to admire him. The narcissist likes people who offer him devotion.

13. He feels very comfortable giving orders because he believes he is the only one who is in possession of the truth. The others seem mediocre, compared to him; they are only mere apprentices or aspirants to be like him.

14. In the face of an argument, they can misrepresent the conversations to make others feel guilty. In order to justify the bad treatment that it gives to others, they look for more or less solvent reasons that excuse their lack of consideration towards others, placing themselves in the best possible situation.

15. Their apparent loquacity facilitates access to others but those friendships lack the intimacy component. Finally, they are perceived as boring conversationalists.

16. Behind its facade, there is a great feeling of incapacity, incompetence, and lack of pleasure in any achievement. Everything they do is aimed at sustaining their fragile self-esteem.

17. The difference between self-esteem and narcissism is according to Bushman and Baumeister (1998): "High self-esteem means thinking well of oneself, while narcissism implies passionately wanting to think well of oneself." So for the narcissist, self-esteem is

the result of external success, what they do not trust is their personal worth.

18. They take great care of their image and their manners since they continuously sit in a shop window. You can demand the same from nearby people, influencing them to behave in a model way and if you don't get it, criticize and ridicule them thinking that it is "for your own good". But if the people around them fulfill their wishes, the narcissist can feel their shadow, so he criticizes them in the same way.

19. Since the image is everything, the situations in which it may be exposed to others or to the possible criticism of these poses a great threat.

20. For your person to look, they exaggerate their merits and minimize those of others.

21. They dismiss emotions such as sadness or anxiety because they think that feeling something like this is "weak." They do not like to talk about their problems or their negative emotions for fear of being seen as a fragile person. They do not like to feel vulnerable since it is a symptom of inferiority. He prefers to offer an image of imperturbability.

22. They have big unrealistic dreams of job success, economic and looking for ideal

romantic love. They also have great fantasies of power.

23. They give great importance to material possessions and in general in everything that implies recognition by others.

24. He presumes to lead a different type of life and this is how he can be involved in insecure businesses, risky sports, lots of sexual conquests, repeated plastic surgery. Whenever there is the possibility of standing out from others, it will.

25. You experience lasting feelings of boredom, of meaninglessness in your lives, of worthlessness, of emptiness, you feel impoverished from an emotional point of view and you crave deeper emotional experiences.

26. It has a sense of corruptible morals and ethics, has changing values and interests, and belittles unusual and conventional valuesand norms. You can show sexual behavior that includes promiscuity, lack of inhibition and marital infidelities.

Chapter 14- Toxic Relationships Recovery

How to Reduce Conflicts in Relationships

Being in touch with your feelings and emotions can be an important way to protect yourself from future abuse. We are doomed to repeat history if we choose not to learn from it. It can be necessary to take a long hard look at your own needs to determine if you are capable of having these needs met within your current relationship. Self-reflection requires honesty. Honesty can be painful, but it is through this pain that we are able to complete a metamorphosis.

This tactic of manipulation can keep victims glued to an abuser's side. Self-love can be a powerful wedge, allowing the abused partner to become the comfort that they're so desperately seeking from the abuser. No matter the outcome, staying or leaving, we must learn to care for ourselves. A person who doesn't value themselves will accept demeaning and degrading behavior because they feel as though they deserve it.

You deserve to be happy. Your situation may feel absolutely hopeless, but I can promise you that you have it within yourself to make any decision you need to in the interest of self-preservation. Admitting to yourself that you're in an abusive relationship can feel a bit like taking a step toward the edge of a cliff that drops into oblivion, an unknown abyss. You know that you are comfortable in this misery, but this isn't happiness.

Taking these next steps takes courage.

Forgiveness

This isn't forgiveness for abuse; that will come later. This is an honest look at the relationship. It is imperative to understand that, as a victim of abuse, you participated in this situation. There is something inside that has been ashamed and afraid to take any ownership of this hardship. Listen, you have wounds that you will need to heal.

There are reasons that you gravitated toward an abusive partner, and that is something that will need to be addressed one day. For now, forgiveness.

You are worthy of attention, love, and kindness. Begin to manifest these things by caring for yourself. Understand that you had a hand in this dynamic and forgive yourself. This is the first step toward trusting yourself again. There are so many ways to process the guilt that we feel in these situations, and you can choose what works for you. Reflection is enough for some, but others find it helpful to write yourself a letter.

Invest in Yourself

Abusive relationships have the potential to rob us of our confidence. Narcissistic partners want you to feel as though you are silly and irrelevant, and your goals do not matter. It is much easier to lord over another person if their spirit is broken. Loving one's self can be the most difficult thing in the world when it feels like everything is against you. Any normal human being dropped in a situation such as this is miserable and dejected.

Make a plan to begin gluing the shattered pieces of yourself back together. This sounds like a huge and abstract undertaking, but it doesn't have to be.

Learning to love yourself again can be as familiar as coming home to an old friend. We are going to take it step by step.

Human beings are uniquely cognizant, which affords us a measure of control over our own lives that the rest of the animal kingdom is missing. Situations (like abusive relationships) can force us into a fishbowl and take away this control. It can be so easy to overlook that we can be exactly what we want to be. We can make it so easy to love ourselves by becoming our own hero. Be the sort of person that you would love and admire.

Make a list of the qualities and values that you want to embody. List goals and milestones that you want to achieve. It can help if you close your eyes and picture a person that you really admire; this person can be a role model or someone that you have completely made up. What makes this person so admirable to you? Independence? Bravery? Fashion sense? There is nothing too silly. You are authoring the next changes that will occur in your own life. This list may have as many entries as you need. The following is an example to use as a template, should you become stumped:

Who I want to Be:

- Creative
- Funny
- Brave

This list is a way for you to take back your self-image from your abusive partner's hands. It is your job to decide who you want to be. You decide what you value, your hair color, your goals, and the way that you handle conflict. You don't have to see yourself through the eyes of someone who is incentivized to keep you down.

Now that you have created your list, break it down entry by entry. This is going to be a map to achieving your goals. Working on your list will give you a project to focus on when the days become dark, and it is a fast-track way to relearn self-love. Creating these lists also inches us closer and closer to self-reliance. Each individual goal from your list is now a new list, with steps that you can take to achieve these things. Example:

Creative:

- Research different creative mediums.

- Buy the sketchbook or supplies needed to begin learning new skills.

- Use art to express anger or sadness.

Experiment with other methods.

There is no goal or quality that cannot be broken down in this way. Take the pen back from your partner and begin writing your own story again. Stimulate these healthy conversations with yourself, because this communication is going to be necessary moving forward.

Find an Outlet

In order to protect yourself from bottling up the words of an abusive partner, it can be important to find an outlet to use for self-expression. Journaling could be a great way to document the abuse and rise above it.

There is a lot of unreleased tension in victims of abuse. Stress and anxiety have become a staple of everyday life. Any moment might bring another fight.

Vent your anger or sadness through a journal or other artistic medium. Allow your mind to rant and rave about the things that you are feeling. Having a way to relieve some of the pressure can be vital in abuse cases. It can also be helpful to find an interest to focus on and is a great way to learn a new skill.

Research

In the same way that you bought this book, begin obsessively consuming material about narcissists, codependents, or abuse. There is a certain mystery to the way that our brains work in these situations. Sometimes we can be unsure of our own actions and motivations. In order to heal, it is necessary to understand.

Demystifying abuse will allow you to pull back the veil shrouding the abuser. The only way that you are going to believe that your partner has something wrong is if you are faced with the facts over and over again. Learn the patterns of abuse and clinical definitions.

Absorbing articles, videos, books, and other literature on the subject will also allow you to predict your partner's next moves. The abusive partner may seem erratic and unpredictable, but there are reasons behind every behavior. Every name that you have ever been called out of malice.

Both narcissists and codependents require validation in the same way. This validation is achieved through manipulation and sometimes name-calling and random fights. A narcissist can seem loving one moment and vile the next, but this is just another part of their process.

Learn everything that you can while you are trapped in this situation. Anticipate the attack and allow the words to roll right off of your skin. When you understand the motivation, then the fights stop seeming so personal.

Exercise

Eating and living in a sedentary way is often related to depression and stress. Take back your wellbeing by taking care of your body. This will help improve the way that you feel physically and your self-esteem. Exercise will also help fight all the negative emotions with the brain chemicals that it produces. Exercising for just thirty minutes a day can drastically allow you to change the way that you see yourself. Abuse will slowly and deviously steal away your confidence and happiness.

Exercise is recommended by doctors to treat both anxiety and depression. Endorphins are released that encourage an overall calm that can combat feelings of negativity brought on by your surroundings. The movement can also induce a meditative state that allows you to forget about the troubles that await you when you return home.

Challenge Your Comfort Zone

When your life feels stale, prison-like, and depressing, it can be difficult to spring back to life. Challenging yourself to escape this comfort zone is hard, but it can also be a very rewarding experience. There are so many volunteer organizations that would love to have assistance. Social activities of this nature may also allow you to find new friends and reestablish a support system.

Your partner will object to these ventures, especially if they are narcissistic. It can be a good idea to shrug off their watchful eye and do some activities that you are interested in. If you are concerned that they will be angry when they find you, remember that they are angry (for sport) constantly anyway. There is no winning, so you might as well take care of your own needs.

Self-soothing

Break free of the abusive trauma bond by becoming the person that you turn to for your own comfort. Do not allow your partner to take away the pain of a fresh fight by becoming a different person right in front of you. Learn tactics to calm yourself down, as this talent has the potential to save you from the bondage of an abusive relationship.

When you need to calm yourself, use cozy blankets in a quiet room. Read a book until your body feels less stressed. Listen to relaxing music or play a podcast to drift along on the tone of a stranger's voice. Sometimes it can even be helpful to just allow yourself to feel the anger and sadness and then go about your day.

Baths are a wonderful way to calm down. Candles can also be helpful. Learn about the things that work to relax you and reach for those the next time you are upset. Abusive partners will dangle comfort over your head so that you bend to their will. Behaviors like this make a narcissist feel powerful. Learn to be your own hero and your own light in the dark.

Praise Yourself

If you are dating a narcissist, then your self-image has been ripped to shreds. The narcissist is doing this for their own gain. Their view of you has nothing to do with who you actually are. Begin to shake off all that negative and toxic commentary and challenge yourself to replace it with words of encouragement. There are so many areas where you excel. You have so many brilliant ideas. You are so resilient.

Next time your partner is calling you names or mocking you, pretend that they are doing these things to a friend.

You would tell that person that the abuser was all wrong and that they are worthy of love. Treat yourself with the same respect.

Stop the Comparison

Comparing yourself to others can add another layer of toxicity on an already toxic sandwich. Your relationship isn't good right now, and there is no need to hold yourself up to someone who has it together at the moment. You are learning some of the most important lessons of your life, and it is already difficult.

Spending too much time on social media can damage your confidence further. Avoid the things that do not make you feel good. Your journey is completely different from those around you. You are dealing with a situation that many people would not be strong enough to make it through.

Time for Yourself

In order to maintain your sanity in the chaos around you, it is necessary for you to spend time doing the things that you love. Music, swimming, hiking, or dancing would all be great examples of activities that allow for escape and relaxation.

It is imperative that you keep your relationship from defining your life.

Your partner may object to you spending time without them around because they would rather you not have the chance to calm down. For your own sanity, do whatever you need to do to go out on your own without your partner. There need to be boundaries set that your partner will not cross.

Activities that allow for reflection can also be a good idea. Meditation and yoga will help to solidify your overall mental health. Learning to keep your center in the face of chaos can be a useful skill to have in these situations.

Therapy

It is not always easy to get to a therapist when you are in an abusive relationship. A professional is going to be the best way to seek help for yourself. Therapy will also allow you to reclaim your sanity and stolen self-esteem. A professional will be able to offer you guidance tailored to your specific situation.

Talking to a professional is the quickest and most effective way to address your mental state and the condition of your relationship.

The therapist will be able to help you see your situation in an objective way. This can also help to restore your self-worth.

Is There Anything to Save?

Use these same eyes to look at your partner. Make a list of qualities that you require in a mate or in a relationship. Things that are important to your overall happiness and wellbeing. Do you want independence within your relationship? Do you want a partner who doesn't lash out in anger?

Objectively, if you are making no excuses for anyone else's behavior, can your partner be the person that you need them to be? Have you been looking at this relationship in rose-colored glasses? Do not allow fleeting moments of kindness to obscure mountains of bad behavior.

Codependency is a deeply rooted behavior that can take lots of effort to change. To save a relationship that is plagued with codependency, both partners must be willing to take steps to change their behavior. Therapy is likely going to be necessary because personal accountability is lacking from the side of the controlling partner. You know your partner better than anyone else, and it is going to take so much honesty to be able to move forward in a way that benefits both parties.

Empathy is the deciding factor. Has your partner ever done anything for you without expecting repayment? Do you believe that your partner is attached to you, or the things that you are able to do for them? These questions are also dependent on the level of control that your partner is exerting upon, because if abuse is involved beyond manipulation, then you need to leave.

If you are involved with a partner that you suspect is a narcissist, things will not change. Empathy is necessary for the relationship to evolve into something that isn't harmful toward both parties. There are extenuating circumstances (such as shared children) that force some victims to continue relationships with narcissist partners. Extensive therapy is needed to keep the abusive partner in check, and these situations involve the victim forgoing a healthy romantic relationship.

Unless children are involved (and usually even if children are involved), the most sensible course of action is to go. Narcissists panic when they have been threatened with being alone. They will not move on until they have found someone that they consider to better. These individuals will pretend that they are going to change their behavior to save the relationship; they may even believe this.

The fact of the matter is that narcissism is a slow poison. Most psychologists that this disorder is incurable and will be a detriment to anyone close to the abuser.

A narcissist will promise change. Their behavior will get better for a few weeks or maybe even a month. They may even want to save the partnership. It isn't possible for these partners to act in opposition to their nature for very long, and their nature is to serve themselves through the oppression of those closest to them. If you are in the blast-zone, then you are always at risk.

How to Know When it's Time to Go

For those in narcissistic relationships, this research is likely a sign that the end is drawing near. You have probably made up your mind already when it comes to the dissolution of your relationship. Most readers of this book are either retroactively reading about their experience or are entering the miserable stage of limbo right before the trigger is pulled. A stage of stagnation where you are left wondering if you will ever find the courage to say the words.

If you are teetering on the edge of singledom, listening to your own body can be a clue to your deeper desires.

Do you still enjoy spending time with your partner? Do you dread being in the same room with your significant other? What does your body tell you about time spent together?

If there is any physical violence in your relationship, the time to go is now or the soonest that you can safely escape. When you are caught in a cycle of abuse, it can be best to make up your mind and wait silently for an opportunity to run. The best thing that you can do for your future is to guard your safety now. Leaving is a provocation and should be done swiftly and quietly. Have people in your life on standby, ready to assist you with your escape when you give the word.

Readers who are involved in codependent relationships must assure that their partner is willing and capable of change. If the offending party is comfortable with the dynamic of the partnership, this is a strong indication that nothing will change. Never feel guilty for taking steps to ensure your own happiness. You are not responsible for the feelings of others. Threats and further attempts at manipulation are a good sign that you are making the right choice.

Those who leave partners who have controlled and belittled them throughout the relationship have this deeply ingrained view that they are unworthy of love. Victims believe that if they leave such a situation, no one else would want them.

Their hobbies, interests, values, and looks have been torn apart for so long that it can be hard for them to see themselves as worthy.

The fights are always manipulated to seem as though the victim is deserving of the abuse. The victim made a tiny mistake, so the abuser is justified in exploding. No matter what the victim does, it will never be enough to stop the flood. If you have found yourself asking your partner to stop criticizing your every move, you may be one of these victims. Do you believe that you have been treated like a partner should be treated? If the answer is no, then it is time to formulate a plan.

Conclusion

Gaslighting is a kind of psychological mistreatment. Somebody who is gaslighting will attempt to make a victim question their impression of the real world. The deceiver may persuade the victim into believing that their recollections aren't right or that they are blowing up over nothing. The abuser may then present their own contemplations and emotions as "the genuine truth." Deceivers/narcissists can cause a lot of injuries.

On the off chance that you are involved with a deceiver/narcissist, it might have damaged you in ways that you aren't truly aware of yet. Contemplate how the deceiver/narcissist might be affecting your perspective on yourself and your general surroundings. Just as being able to speak your feelings helps you connect with them—and with the energy to stand up for yourself—so does expressing your feelings in a different way.

Gaslighting is the favorite tool of a narcissist, and a narcissist will seek to keep you under control by gradually eroding every bit of your sanity. Doubting your own senses is in no way healthy for you, and you have to be aware of how narcissists operate to avoid the mess of dealing with them in your future relationships.

Millions and millions of people around the world are finding their real voice against gaslighting and are now enlightening more people about the damaging effects of gaslighting. It is no understatement when I repeat that countless people have fallen victim to this form of abuse at one point or the other in their lives.

The good news is there are countless survivors who have fought their way through depression and other devastating effects of gaslighting and are now living healthy lives. I believe that with the proper management techniques, any victim can get over the emotional abuse and mental manipulation to go on and lead a productive and fulfilling life.

My thoughts are with you, and you can find strength in the fact that you can make it through the trying times. Use that strength to carry yourself through until you find your true self again.

The next step is to get all the help you can, find a support group, and start making plans for your own self.

So please, remember that Inner Strength + Emotional Support + Plan = Independence and Freedom.

Made in the USA
Columbia, SC
23 July 2020